Democracy's Big Day

Democracy's Big Day

The Inauguration of our President
1789–2009

Jim Bendat

iUniverse Star
New York Lincoln Shanghai

Democracy's Big Day
The Inauguration of our President 1789–2009

iUniverse Star
an iUniverse, Inc. imprint

iUniverse books may be ordered through booksellers or by contacting:

iUniverse
2021 Pine Lake Road, Suite 100
Lincoln, NE 68512
www.iuniverse.com
1-800-Authors (1-800-288-4677)

Because of the dynamic nature of the Internet, any Web addresses or links contained in this book may have changed since publication and may no longer be valid.

The views expressed in this work are solely those of the author and do not necessarily reflect the views of the publisher, and the publisher hereby disclaims any responsibility for them.

ISBN: 978-1-58348-466-1 (pbk)
ISBN: 978-0-595-88948-8 (cloth)
ISBN: 978-0-595-88502-2 (ebk)

Printed in the United States of America

Contents

Preface

The day before the 2005 U.S. Presidential Inauguration, I visited the National Archives in Washington, D.C. The Bible that George Washington had used at our nation's first inauguration, in 1789, was on display. There was a note next to the old book, relating its history and mentioning that four other presidents—Warren G. Harding, in 1921; Dwight D. Eisenhower, in 1953; Jimmy Carter, in 1977; and George Bush, in 1989—had used that very Bible when they had been inaugurated in subsequent ceremonies. The note further stated that George W. Bush had also planned to place his hand upon that Bible in 2001, but bad weather had prevented him from being able to do so.

I was stunned. Before the 2001 ceremony, every media outlet in the country had reported that Bush was going to use the George Washington Bible. The *Washington Post* ran a detailed story about the Bible being transported via train from New York to Washington so that it could be used at the ceremony. During one of my pre-inauguration interviews on national television, I had said the same thing. On Inauguration Day that year, not one network mentioned that the inclement weather had forced a change in plans. The next day, no newspaper reported that the old Bible had not been used. Consequently, I wrote that George W. Bush had indeed used it at his first inauguration.

Another part of that note next to the Bible in the National Archives also bothered me: why didn't it mention that Zachary Taylor had also used the George Washington Bible at the 1849 Inauguration? That was a piece of information I had learned from a 1965 book on inauguration history, and I had repeated it in my own book on the subject.

This is the third edition of my book of vignettes on U.S. Presidential Inauguration Day history. The first edition, *Democracy's Big Day*, was published in 2000. It was the first book written on the subject since 1971. The second book, *Democracy's Big Day 2005 Edition*, was published in 2004. Each book has been written for readers of all ages and has been designed to make history fun. I have never intended the books to serve as treatises on the subject. Nevertheless, it has been my desire for my work to reflect the most accurate information ever written on inauguration history.

In the pursuit of accuracy, I constantly considered a number of questions that I don't suppose a lot of people think about often: Who was sworn into office indoors? Who affirmed the oath? Who was sworn in on consecutive days? What was the weather for each ceremony? What role have women played in inaugural history? For every question, I needed an answer.

So, what about that note at the National Archives? For me, it was time to search for the truth. I contacted the St. John's Masonic Lodge in New York City, which normally houses the George Washington Bible. After a number of e-mails and phone calls, I had a lengthy discussion with Jules Garfunkel, one of the lodge members who had brought the Bible to Washington in 2001. He kindly gave me the full story behind the last-minute decision to not use the Bible during the ceremony that year, the details of which are located here in the chapter called "A Biblical Journey."

Another lodge member, Piers A. Vaughan, furnished the correct information on Zachary Taylor. As it turns out, the source from the 1965 book was wrong. The George Washington Bible was *not* used at Taylor's inauguration. Rather, it was used at Taylor's funeral, in 1850.

Since the publication of my second book, I also read a transcript of a speech by an historian who stated that Franklin Pierce was one of two presidents to have affirmed the oath of office, rather than using the more customary words, "I do solemnly swear." In both of my books, I had indicated that Pierce had been the only one to affirm it. Had I botched that one, too? The historian did not indicate the name of the other president, and I wanted to know who it was. I contacted that historian. He advised me that the other president to affirm the oath was Herbert Hoover—presumably because he was a Quaker.

I then contacted Matt Schaefer and Lynn Smith at the Herbert Hoover Presidential Library in Iowa. That library provided me with much of the information that is in the chapter entitled "Let's Hear It for the Girl." I also learned that the Hoover Library has a newsreel from the 1929 Inauguration, a sound film that includes Hoover's swearing-in. It is the best possible evidence of his oath of office. The phrase "solemnly swear" was a part of Hoover's oath; the word "affirm" was never used. Reprieve granted.

Then there was the matter of whether George Washington really added the words "so help me God" after he recited the oath of office in 1789. I had previously fallen into the trap of simply accepting that Washington had said those words, solely because other historians had said so, but I came to realize the issue is not so clear. Another "so help me God" question arose when I became aware that another historian was claiming that Franklin D. Roosevelt did not add those words after reciting the oath at his first inauguration in 1933. This particular historian indicated that Roosevelt was so anxious about his forthcoming inaugural address that he forgot to say "so help me God." But again, there are recordings from that 1933 ceremony. The fact is Roosevelt didn't forget anything; he did indeed recite the words "so help me God" at the conclusion of the oath.

It is certainly not unusual for a writer's claims to be challenged. When I found a discrepancy between my words and those of others, you can see how I then checked out each new issue. The search for the truth continues. I hope I got everything right this time!

Jim Bendat
Los Angeles, California

P.S. Throughout the book, I have made a conscious decision to refer to our nation's 41st president as George Bush, not "George H.W. Bush" as many people now seem to call him. He was always called George Bush during his presidency, and his presidential library is officially called the George Bush Presidential Library and Museum. Historians have never confused John Adams with John Quincy Adams. I am similarly confident that we should be able to distinguish George Bush from George W. Bush.

Foreword

There are few events in the world that symbolize the essence of democracy more than the inauguration of a United States president. It stands as one of the few events in world politics that has remained essentially unchanged. In *Democracy's Big Day*, Jim Bendat paints a vivid picture of not only the process, but also of the traditions, quirks, and unusual events connected with this two-century-old institution.

Bendat's fascination with presidential politics goes back to his childhood. In 1960, as a twelve year old, he attended, with his grandfather, the Democratic Convention in his hometown of Los Angeles where Sen. John F. Kennedy was nominated for president. That began his lifelong interest. Eight years later, in 1968, Bendat, then a student at Northwestern University, attended both national conventions. He first traveled to Miami to witness the nomination of Richard Nixon at the Republican Convention. Then, he was in Chicago when the Democrats met to nominate Vice President Hubert Humphrey—one of the most tumultuous nominating conventions in United States history.

I actually played a small but key role in Bendat's desire to write this book. In 1993, I traveled to Washington to cover the inauguration of Bill Clinton, and Jim asked me to bring back an official program for him. Bendat, a longtime collector of sports memorabilia, suddenly became interested in collecting programs from other, previous inaugurations. As he obtained these programs, he realized that there was a rich history of stories that made each inauguration a unique event. That is how the idea of *Democracy's Big Day* was born.

Jim Bendat, who in his daily life has worked as a public defender in Los Angeles for more than three decades, began a journey that would lead to museums, libraries, archivists, and anyone who might have some insight about a particular inauguration. This devotion to detail led him to the Museum of Television and Radio in Beverly Hills, to watch, on videotape or kinescope, virtually every minute of every inauguration since Dwight D. Eisenhower's, in 1953.

We all know the basics of any inauguration—the oath of office, the inaugural address, the 21-gun salute. What we see in *Democracy's Big Day* are the stories within the event itself—how certain traditions were born, the interaction between incoming and outgoing presidents, how personal preferences of the new presidents played a role in their inauguration. These insights, which are often overlooked, give a vivid picture of inaugurations, beginning with George Washington in 1789, and continuing through George W. Bush in 2005.

Bendat's exhaustive desire for accuracy has led him to uncover that certain details, previously generally accepted to be fact, were incorrect.

Only one thing was missing when Bendat wrote his first edition of *Democracy's Big Day* in 2000—he had never attended an inauguration in person. That all changed in 2001 when he attended George W. Bush's first inauguration, and continued in 2005 when he witnessed George W. Bush's second inaugural. Bendat's expertise was called upon in both those years, and he helped provide commentary in news reports and live coverage for a variety of news organizations, including CBS, CNN, Fox News Channel, MSNBC, ABC, ITV, and BBC Radio.

What began as a simple fascination has grown into a successful series of books and has turned Bendat into one of the foremost authorities on presidential inaugurations.

It has turned *Democracy's Big Day* into Jim Bendat's Big Day as well.

Steve Futterman
CBS News

Democracy's Big Day

Our national election for president of the United States occurs every four years. It always takes place in November, in a leap year, in the year of the Summer Olympic Games. Then, about two-and-a-half months later, on January 20, in Washington, D.C., there is a celebration honoring the new president. It is our nation's presidential inauguration. The world watches as our country passes the title and power of the presidency from one person to another in a peaceful and orderly manner. It is a big and colorful show, with red, white, and blue banners flying everywhere. The city hosts a formal ceremony, a big parade, and a number of gala inaugural balls.

People across our nation watch the event. More than a million spectators line the streets of Washington, hoping to catch a part of history. In our homes and schools, Americans gather to see the spectacle on television. In 1989, President George Bush specifically mentioned our young citizens when he said, in his inaugural address, "Our children are watching in schools throughout our great land. And to them I say, thank you for watching democracy's big day. For a democracy belongs to us all, and freedom is like a beautiful kite that can go higher and higher with the breeze."

Changes in power in other countries can often be quite different. We have heard of revolutions, takeovers, and military juntas that seize power in other parts of the world. Some nations hold an election, while many do not. In those nations where an election is held, it can take place at any given time of the year, sometimes upon very short notice to the population. In other nations, bitterness, mistrust, and chaos often follow close elections. After a disputed election in Mexico in 2006, chair throwing and fistfights between supporters and opponents of the new leader marred that country's presidential inauguration.

Our country's November election may also have been a bitter one, marked by numerous differences between the political parties. But in the January inauguration, the same people who had previously battled one another might well now be sitting on the inaugural platform together or marching in the inaugural parade next to one another.

The 2000 election was such an example. George W. Bush and Al Gore did not know the result of their election until the United States Supreme Court rendered a 5-4 decision in favor of Bush a full five weeks after the voting had ended. When President Bush was inaugurated the following month, outgoing Vice President Gore was sitting just a few feet away. In his inaugural address, Bush thanked Gore "for a contest conducted with spirit and ended with grace." Bush then expressed confidence that "Republicans and Democrats will come together to do what's right for America."

His words of reconciliation were in keeping with the reminder of Abraham Lincoln. "When an election is over," Lincoln said, "it is altogether fitting a free people that until the next election they should be one people." Or, as President John F. Kennedy began his inaugural address, "We observe today not a victory of party, but a celebration of freedom."

Indeed, our Inauguration Day is one that demonstrates the continuity of our country and the renewal of the democratic process, as well as the healing that is sometimes needed after an election battle. There was perhaps no better example of this healing process than President Ronald Reagan's immediately appointing the outgoing president, Jimmy Carter—a man Reagan had soundly defeated in the November election—to be his representative to greet fifty-two American hostages who had been released from captivity in Iran on the same day as the 1981 Inauguration.

A different, but still very significant example of a nation's healing occurred when Chief Justice Edward D. White swore in President Woodrow Wilson, in 1913. The *New York Times* described the event as "a remarkable illustration of what American institutions really mean—a man born in the South took the oath as president, and it was administered by a man who fifty years ago was in arms against the Government. Chief Justice White is the first ex-Confederate soldier to swear in a President of the United States. This oath was administered by a Catholic to a Presbyterian. There are other countries in which such a thing would be difficult to understand."

George Washington's, in 1789, was the first such presidential inauguration. Our next president's ceremony, on January 20, 2009, is officially called the "Fifty-sixth Presidential Inauguration" because it is the fifty-sixth such planned ceremony. But there have actually been more than fifty-six such occasions. In our country, whether there is a big ceremony or not, whenever a person has recited the presidential oath of office as prescribed in the United States Constitution, that person has been inaugurated as president. In fact, the 2009 Inauguration commemorates the seventy-first time in our nation's history that the oath has been administered to a president.

The vast majority of inaugurations have been happy and festive occasions. But others have been solemn and sad events. One took place after the previous president resigned his post because of a major scandal. On eight occasions, a vice president has succeeded to the presidency because of the death of his predecessor. These sudden inaugurations have taken place in some unusual places, ranging from an airplane in Dallas, Texas, to an old home in Plymouth Notch, Vermont, where an old kerosene lamp provided the only light in the night.

Other inaugurations took on somber tones because of the conditions in our country and the world at that particular time. But the number of truly significant inaugurations probably number fewer than ten: George Washington's, in 1789, at the close of our Revolutionary War; Thomas Jefferson's, in 1801, representing the first change in American political power; Andrew Jackson's, in 1829, when the masses of people took over power for the first time; Abraham Lincoln's, in 1861, on the eve of civil war; Rutherford B. Hayes's, in 1877, and George W. Bush's, in 2001, after disputed elections; Woodrow Wilson's, in 1917, on the eve of the United States entering a world war; and Franklin D. Roosevelt's, in 1933 and 1945, in the midst of the Great Depression and in the middle of World War II. Those were truly inaugurations of significance.

Fortunately, most inaugurations are just plain fun! An article was published in the 1901 Inauguration program predicting what our inauguration would be like in the year 2001. The article predicted that our new president that year would be from the state of Ontario and that he would have been elected to serve a term of eight years. There would be 118 states in our country. The inaugural parade would be thirty-six miles in length and would include marchers parading in "ancient vehicles known as automobiles, locomobiles, and glides." The president would review the parade from an "air ship." Later in the evening, guests would arrive at the inaugural ball via "private air yachts."

In reality, of course, 2001 did not quite turn out to be so futuristic. But our next Inauguration Day will continue to help fill our history books with wonderful new stories from democracy's big day. This book recites that history by going through this one big day in the life of our nation's new president. Each section of the book will represent a part of that day: the early morning hours when the new president calls upon his predecessor at the White House, the taking of the oath and the inaugural address at the Capitol, the inaugural parade in the afternoon, and the inaugural balls at night. Each section will begin by previewing what our new president might expect to occur during that part of the day, followed by a series of vignettes from the past about that particular aspect of our inauguration process.

So, let the big day begin!

I

The Prelude

Morning Glory

There is exhilaration in the air on the morning of Inauguration Day. The official festivities will begin shortly before noon at the Capitol, with the new president's swearing-in set for exactly twelve o'clock, but there is still much to be done before then by both the outgoing president and the president-elect.

At the White House, the president may have a few last-minute bills to sign or letters to write. He may choose to exercise his power of executive clemency by issuing last-minute pardons or commutations to people in legal trouble. He will say good-bye to the staff at the White House and thank them for all their contributions to his administration. By tradition, he will also write a note to his successor, wishing the new president and first lady (or first gentleman, once a female president is elected) good luck in their new jobs and at their new home.

The president-elect is busy getting ready to assume the awesome responsibilities of our country's new chief executive. Congratulatory greetings are pouring in from all over the world. The president-elect might receive a national security briefing from the departing president's advisors and might also find a little time to take a brisk jog along Pennsylvania Avenue, as Bill Clinton did on his inauguration morning in 1993.

Around 9 a.m., the president-elect and spouse will go to a national prayer service. At George Washington's first inauguration, in 1789, a church service was part of the inauguration ceremony itself; but that was the only time it was an official inaugural event. Now, the new president does so by tradition on Inauguration Day. Beginning with Franklin D. Roosevelt, in 1933, most presidents have attended the service at St. John's Episcopal Church, which is next to the White House. There are churches of virtually every possible denomination in Washington. In both 1993 and 1997, Bill Clinton went to services at the predominantly African American Metropolitan AME Church, a congregation that had deep roots in the civil rights movement. The moving service and beautiful music brought him to tears.

Between 10:00 and 10:30 a.m., the president-elect and family will be driven to the White House for the traditional meeting of the old and the new, a tradition that began in 1877 with Ulysses S. Grant and Rutherford B. Hayes. The president and first lady will be waiting at the north portico entrance to greet them. Everyone will pose for pictures. The families will then have some private time together, while enjoying juice, coffee and pastries. In 1993, George and Barbara Bush's dog, Millie, was also outside to greet Bill and Hillary Clinton and their daughter, Chelsea. "Welcome to your new house, Chelsea," said President Bush, as the twelve-year-old petted Millie.

Four years earlier, President-elect Bush had summarized his inauguration morning in his agenda book in his own rather precise way: "6 a.m.—catch 3 news shows. Drink coffee—Play with grand kids—Pray—Go to WHouse—Get Sworn in."

Indeed, after about an hour, sometime between 11:00 and 11:30, everyone will leave the White House and begin the procession up to the Capitol. The president and president-elect will drive together. By tradition, the outgoing president will sit on the right side in the rear passenger seat, while the new president will be on the left side. This is a practice that began in 1837 when President Andrew Jackson rode to the Capitol together with President-elect Martin Van Buren in an elegant carriage, one that had been constructed from original oak beams from the ship

President William Howard Taft and President-elect Woodrow Wilson on their way to the Capitol on Inauguration Day, 1913. By tradition, the outgoing president sits on the right side of the vehicle (or, in this instance, a carriage), and the new president is on the left side. **Library of Congress,** Prints and Photographs Division, reproduction number LC-USZ62-67446.

Constitution. The first president and president-elect to take this route in an automobile were Woodrow Wilson and Warren G. Harding, in 1921. The first lady and her successor will drive together in a separate car. The vice president and vice president-elect will also drive together.

In 1809, President-elect James Madison traveled to the Capitol under an escort of volunteer cavalry. He had invited President Thomas Jefferson to ride with him to the Capitol, but Jefferson had politely declined, saying that he felt that such togetherness might "divide the honors of the day." No president is likely to decline such an invitation today, for the image of the outgoing president and the incoming president riding together to the inauguration ceremony is one that demonstrates how our country remains united, even after a recent election in which the two individuals might not have always been so cordial.

There will be many people along the sidewalks of Pennsylvania Avenue as the procession proceeds. The spectators cheer, and the president and president-elect wave to them. Hopefully, the scene is not like it was before Abraham Lincoln's inauguration in 1861, Woodrow Wilson's in 1917, or George W. Bush's in 2005 when armed federal troops and sharpshooters were lining many streets and rooftops due to concerns surrounding the Civil War, World War I, and potential terrorist attacks. In fact, Lincoln felt the need to arrive in Washington before his first inauguration, at night and in disguise.

If this day is like most of our Inauguration Days, all will be festive. Anticipation is building mightily, for the Capitol is only a mile and a half away and the ceremony will soon commence.

The People's Presidents

A number of presidents in our history have won their elections by overwhelming margins. Many of them were very popular and were elected to second terms or even, in the case of Franklin D. Roosevelt, a third and fourth term. But two presidents stand out above all the others in the manner of adulation they received in the months and days just prior to their inaugurations. George Washington and Andrew Jackson were the "people's presidents" who were given huge receptions during the days leading up to their inaugurations as well as emotional farewells at the end of their terms of office.

In 1789, General George Washington took two weeks to travel from his home at Mt. Vernon, Virginia, to New York City, the temporary capital of our new nation. He rode through Alexandria, Georgetown, Washington, Philadelphia, and Baltimore; it seemed as if, every step of the way, tumultuous applause greeted him. There were banners and banquets and receiving lines for the general wherever he went. He arrived in New York City aboard a magnificent ship. Here was a hero of the Revolutionary War who was on his way to becoming our country's first president.

Washington's reaction was not quite as enthusiastic. He had been looking forward to his last years at Mt. Vernon, but he felt obligated to serve his country when asked. He wrote to an old friend that his steps "toward the Presidential chair were like those of a criminal going to the place of execution."

On the day of the ceremony itself, Washington was escorted by carriage from the residence of New York Governor George Clinton, a man who would later serve as vice president under both Thomas Jefferson and James Madison. Washington went to Federal Hall, at the corner of Broad and Wall Streets. There, he was taken to the balcony where he would be sworn into office before a large crowd of people watching from every open window and from the streets below.

General Andrew Jackson's journey from Nashville to Washington in 1829 was triumphant, similar to what Washington had experienced in 1789. He and his followers had overcome the bitterness of a disputed election loss in 1824, when a vote of the House of Representatives had given that year's election to John Quincy Adams. Now, the outsider from Tennessee had finally won the presidency, and his supporters were jubilant.

On the day of the inauguration, a group of veterans gave Jackson an escort to the Capitol. It was said that "the avenue was crowded with carriages of every description, from the splendid Baronet and coach down to wagons and carts, filled with women and children, some in finery and some in rags, for it was the People's President." The crowd was the biggest yet for an inauguration, the first to be held at the east portico of the Capitol. "I have never seen such a crowd before," wrote Daniel Webster. "People have come from five hundred miles to see General Jackson and they really seem to think that the country is rescued from some dreadful danger."

The popularity of Washington and Jackson would continue throughout their terms in office. Their successors were John Adams, in 1797, and Martin Van Buren, in 1837. But both Adams and Van Buren would be overshadowed on their Inauguration Day by the affection that the people still showed for Washington and Jackson. In both of those years, most of the cheers (and some tears as well) from the crowds of people were bestowed upon the beloved, retiring presidents. About his Inauguration Day, John Adams is reported to have said, "A solemn scene it was indeed, and it was made more affecting by the presence of General Washington, whose countenance was as serene and unclouded as the day. He seemed to enjoy a triumph over me. Methought I heard him say, 'Ay! I am fairly out and you are fairly in! See which one of us will be the happiest.'"

Adams's feelings about the office never changed. Even when his son, John Quincy Adams, became president in 1825, Adams stated, "No man who ever held the office of president would congratulate a friend on obtaining it."

Can't We All Get Along?

The orderly change in leadership from one president to another is truly a model for all nations. Most presidents and presidents-elect have been extremely courteous to one another. In 1853, President Millard Fillmore took this cordiality to a new level in the gracious manner with which he greeted his successor, Franklin Pierce. The Fillmores entertained Pierce at dinner, and the president took Pierce to a lecture on English humorists, as well as a trip along the Potomac River to inspect a new ship. It is possible that Fillmore's kindness may have had something to do with Pierce and his wife's recent tragedy of seeing their eleven-year-old son, Benjamin, die in a train crash, the third child they had lost. Mrs. Pierce, still overcome with grief, had decided not to come to Washington for the inauguration, and the president-elect was thus alone.

Nevertheless, Washington Irving wrote at the time:

> It was admirable to see the quiet and courtesy with which this great transition of power and rule from one party to another took place. I was at festive meetings where the members of the opposite parties mingled socially together, and have seen the two Presidents arm-in-arm as if the sway of an immense empire was not passing from one to another.

But not all presidents, or presidents-elect, have handled themselves with such gracious dignity. For example, neither John Adams, in 1801, nor his son John Quincy Adams, in 1829, seems to have been a very good loser.

Neither of them attended the inauguration of his successor. John Adams was bitter about his election loss and considered Thomas Jefferson a radical, while John Quincy Adams, as well as many in the Washington establishment, considered Andrew Jackson and his followers to be lowlifes.

In 1869, President Andrew Johnson refused to ride in the carriage to the Capitol with his successor, Ulysses S. Grant. The feeling was actually mutual, as Grant didn't want Johnson in his carriage. Instead, Grant's chief of staff, John Rawlings, sat next to the general. Johnson then decided not to participate in the ceremony at all. So, while Grant was at the Capitol being sworn in, Johnson stayed at the White House, quietly signing a few bills for the last time as president.

In 1933, President-elect Franklin D. Roosevelt broke with tradition when he remained in the car at the north portico of the White House, waiting for President Herbert Hoover to join him for the procession to the Capitol. Hoover took the automobile ride with Roosevelt; but when Roosevelt tried to speak with him, Hoover just looked straight ahead, ignoring his successor. Roosevelt then decided to grin and wave to the crowd on the way to the Capitol. Again, Hoover just looked straight ahead and barely said a word. The next morning's *New York Times* described Roosevelt as "vivid and animated" and Hoover as "clothed in a rigidity which held him during most of the ceremony. Down all Pennsylvania Avenue, he was in the position of one who listens politely, but almost disinterestedly to the conversation of a companion."

But all inaugurations pale in comparison with the lack of harmony exhibited between outgoing President Harry S. Truman and President-elect Dwight D. Eisenhower in 1953. The two men had many disagreements during the 1952 campaign, which had resulted in Eisenhower's victory over Democrat Adlai E. Stevenson. On inauguration morning, there was even some question as to whether Truman would pick up Eisenhower at the general's hotel or whether Eisenhower would make the traditional visit to the White House prior to the procession to the Capitol.

President Herbert Hoover and President-elect Franklin D. Roosevelt had little to say to each other during their ride to the Capitol in 1933. **Architect of the Capitol.**

Truman refused to change tradition and, when asked if he would drive with Eisenhower, the president's response was, "No, General Eisenhower will accompany me. I will still be the president." Upon learning that Truman would not come to his hotel, Eisenhower felt no choice but to go to the White House. But, once he arrived there at around 11:30, the president-elect refused to leave his car and greet Truman. After a number of minutes of waiting, Truman then exited the White House, shook Eisenhower's hand, and the two drove off to the Capitol.

A number of Truman and Eisenhower's campaign disputes had been over the issue of the war in Korea. Eisenhower's son John was a West Point officer, stationed in Korea. For Inauguration Day, John had been pulled off the front lines and brought to Washington so that he could have the opportunity of watching his father sworn in. Eisenhower felt that someone was trying to embarrass him by giving his son special privileges. "That makes me look bad," Eisenhower said to Truman. "Who is the damn fool who brought my son back?" According to Eisenhower, Truman's terse response was, "I did."

In his autobiography, Truman recounted the same conversation. When Eisenhower asked the question about who brought his son home, Truman says his answer was, "The president of the United States ordered your son to attend your inauguration. The president thought it was right and proper for your son to witness the swearing-in of his father to the presidency. If you think someone was trying to embarrass you by this order, then the president assumes full responsibility."

Even the first ladies sometimes have a problem on the short journey from the White House to the Capitol. In 1981, Rosalynn Carter rode with Nancy Reagan. In the car with them was Congressman John Rhodes. "Thank God, John was with us," Mrs. Reagan later wrote, "because he kept up a steady stream of conversation in a very awkward situation. Rosalynn just looked out the window and didn't say a word. I didn't know what to say, so I kept quiet, too. Fortunately, it's a short ride."

II

The Ceremony

Capitol Hill

The procession from the White House to Capitol Hill takes only a handful of minutes. Everyone exits the automobiles and goes inside the magnificent Capitol building. There are a number of offices there, and the president-elect is escorted into one of them to relax for a few moments before the ceremony actually begins.

The great crowd of people outside the west front of the Capitol will see the inauguration platform begin to fill with dignitaries. Members of the United States Senate and House of Representatives will slowly proceed from inside the various parts of the Capitol building, through the Capitol Rotunda, then outside where the crowd awaits them. The chief justice and other members of the U.S. Supreme Court, members of the president's cabinet, and governors of the states will follow them. Military personnel and ambassadors and ministers of foreign countries will also make their way onto the platform.

Because there will be such a large throng of spectators, many of them will only be able to view the proceedings on big video boards. People in the faraway standing-room areas might not even be able to see those screens. There will be many loudspeakers in the area, so everyone should at least be able to hear what is taking place. The first time that such amplified sound was used at an inauguration was at Warren G. Harding's ceremony in 1921. Until then, the only people who had been able to hear anything had been the lucky ones who were within about ten yards of the podium.

The big event is being broadcast around the world. There is a huge stand housing members of the press directly in front of the inauguration stage. This type of coverage has grown greatly over the years. The first inauguration to be communicated elsewhere had taken place in 1845, when James K. Polk's ceremony was reported by telegraph. James Buchanan's inauguration in 1857 was the first one to be photographed. The first ceremony to be filmed and recorded with sound was William McKinley's in 1897. Milestone events in the twentieth century occurred in 1925, when Calvin Coolidge's inauguration was the first to be broadcast on radio, and at Harry S. Truman's ceremony in 1949, the first time the event was ever televised.

The outgoing first lady and the wife of the outgoing vice president will soon join the group on the inauguration platform, followed almost immediately by the spouses of the new president and vice president.

The band will then play "Hail to the Chief" as the outgoing president and vice president come forward. It is the final time that this song will be played in that president's honor. Then, the vice president-elect moves onto the platform.

The trumpets will blare as the president-elect emerges from inside the Capitol to the great cheers of the crowd. When President Theodore Roosevelt stepped onto the inaugural stand in 1905, a "mixed chorus of five hundred voices" greeted him. The band will play a patriotic tune, perhaps John Philip Sousa's "Stars and Stripes Forever," maybe even "Hail to the Chief," even though a president-elect would not yet be our chief executive. Our country's new leader takes a seat near the podium, next to the vice president-elect and their predecessors.

The ceremony begins shortly after 11:30 a.m. with the band playing a medley of patriotic music. Our national anthem is usually heard at the end of the ceremony, but it's sometimes at the beginning. The band might play it, or it might be performed by someone such as famed soprano Marian Anderson, who sang the first and second verses of "The Star Spangled Banner" at both Dwight D. Eisenhower's second inauguration, in 1957, and John F. Kennedy's 1961 ceremony.

There will then be an invocation, the first of a few prayers that are generally delivered at various times during the ceremony. More music is played. Poetry has been read on a few occasions—by Robert Frost, in 1961; Maya Angelou, in 1993; and Miller Williams, in 1997.

The vice president-elect will be called upon to be sworn into office, and he can choose anyone to administer the oath. In 1997, Associate Justice Ruth Bader Ginsburg of the United States Supreme Court swore in Albert Gore. In 2005, Speaker of the House J. Dennis Hastert swore in Richard Cheney. Similarly, Speaker Sam Rayburn administered the vice-presidential oath to Hubert Humphrey in 1965, and Speaker Thomas P. "Tip" O'Neill swore in Walter Mondale in 1977. There have also been many occasions when the outgoing vice president swore in his successor. For example, William A. Wheeler swore in Chester A. Arthur in 1881, and Charles G. Dawes did the same for Charles Curtis in 1929. This practice actually remained a very common one through 1945, when outgoing Vice President Henry Wallace administered the oath to Harry S. Truman.

The new vice president raises his right arm as the oath is recited. In 1901, however, the new vice president was Theodore Roosevelt, who had only a few years earlier been a hero of the Spanish-American War, serving as the colonel of a cavalry commonly called the Rough Riders. When it was time for Roosevelt to take his oath, he raised his right hand against his right eyebrow and his palm facing down toward his shoulder. The next day's *New York Times* reported that his salute was "evidently thoroughly unconscious, and thoroughly characteristic of Theodore Roosevelt."

There have been a few other times when the vice-presidential ceremony hasn't followed normal protocol. In 1905, Charles W. Fairbanks was asked if he promised to accept the duties of his office. Instead of answering the question verbally, Fairbanks merely nodded his head. In 1953, Richard Nixon forgot to repeat the word "support" in the part of the vice-presidential oath where he was supposed to promise to "support and defend the Constitution of the United States." While being sworn in, Vice President Lyndon B. Johnson similarly botched part of the oath in 1961. Rather than saying he would accept his post "without any mental reservation or purpose of evasion," Johnson simply said, "without any mental reservation whatever." In Fairbanks's, Nixon's and Johnson's instances, however, no one seemed to notice or care.

The chief justice of the United States will then be called upon to administer the oath of office to the new president of the United States. The trumpets will again sound. The great moment has arrived!

This I Swear

A new president recites the thirty-five words found in Article II, Section 1 of the U.S. Constitution in order to officially become our nation's leader:

> I do solemnly swear (or affirm) that I will faithfully execute the office of President of the United States, and will, to the best of my ability, preserve, protect and defend the Constitution of the United States.

The first person to take this oath was George Washington on April 30, 1789. He had been escorted to Federal Hall in New York City, the temporary seat of our new government. The first swearing-in took place on a balcony of that building, allowing citizens crowding the streets below to be able to view the historic event.

There was a table covered with red velvet, and a Bible was lying on a velvet cushion. There was no United States Supreme Court yet, so Chancellor Robert R. Livingston of the New York judiciary administered the oath to Washington, as our new nation's leader raised his right hand. There is a legend that when the thirty-five words were over, Washington added the words, "I swear, so help me God." Livingston then loudly proclaimed to all who could hear, "It is done. Long live George Washington, president of the United States!" Bells then rang out across the city, and our country thus had its first president.

"Washington's Inauguration—1789" is artist Allyn Cox's depiction of the nation's first inaugural ceremony that took place on the balcony of New York City's Federal Hall. **Architect of the Capitol.**

There are no contemporary accounts indicating that Washington actually said "so help me God," but those words have come to be a virtual part of the oath. The chief justice now always says them, and the new president does so as well, but this custom was not always the practice. Newspaper articles from 1881 indicate that Chester A. Arthur recited the words "so help me God" that year, and almost all presidents in the twentieth and twenty-first centuries have done the same. Yet, a sound film of Herbert Hoover's 1929 swearing-in is evidence that he was a president who did not add those words. A president also has the option of saying "I affirm" rather than "I swear," but the only president to ever *affirm* the oath was Franklin Pierce, in 1853.

The Father of the Inauguration

Almost all of our presidents have participated in an inauguration as both an incoming and outgoing president. Fourteen presidents first served as vice president, and therefore recited different oaths in different ceremonies. Dwight D. Eisenhower and William Howard Taft were involved in multiple inaugurations in unique ways. When Eisenhower was a young cadet at West Point, he marched in the parade at Woodrow Wilson's 1913 Inauguration—forty years before his own inauguration as president.

In that same year, 1913, Taft's term as president ended. A little more than eight years later, he was appointed chief justice of the United States Supreme Court. Then, in 1925 and 1929, Taft was on the other side of the inaugural oath when he swore in Calvin Coolidge and Herbert Hoover.

But James Madison probably holds the most distinguished place among the presidents who have had different roles in our inauguration history. Well before he became the nation's fourth president, Madison had earned the nickname "Father of the Constitution," by virtue of his speeches, effective negotiations, and successful compromises at the Constitutional Convention in 1787.

Part of the work at that convention involved the writing of a president's inaugural oath. An early version simply stated, "I do solemnly swear (or affirm) that I will faithfully execute the office of President of the United States of America." But Madison and fellow Virginia delegate

George Mason believed that the nation's chief executive should also be required to make a promise to support the words and meaning of the Constitution. So, on August 27, 1787, Madison and Mason moved to add to the oath the phrase, "and will, to the best of my judgment and power, preserve, protect, and defend the Constitution of the United States."

Less than three weeks later, the state representatives finalized the oath's wording. They kept almost all of Madison and Mason's amendment, changing only the words "judgment and power" to "ability." It was clear that Madison had made a major contribution to the very oath he would himself recite many years later, at his 1809 and 1813 Inaugurations.

With his 1809 ceremony also featuring the first official inaugural parade, and the first official inaugural ball, it would seem appropriate to call Madison not only the "Father of the Constitution," but also the "Father of the Inauguration."

Where's the Chief?

By tradition, it is the chief justice of the United States who administers the oath of office to the new president. George Washington's inauguration in 1789 was one of the few times when someone other than the chief justice performed the administration of the oath of office. In fact, Washington is the only elected president who was never sworn in by a chief justice. On the day of his second inauguration, in Philadelphia in 1793, Chief Justice John Jay was out of the country. So, United States Supreme Court Associate Justice William Cushing swore in Washington instead.

The first chief justice to have the honor was Oliver Ellsworth at John Adams's inauguration in 1797. John Marshall was the chief justice who administered the oath the most times, a total of nine, from 1801 through 1833.

Aside from Washington's two inaugurations, every other time that the oath has been administered by someone other than the chief justice has been at the sudden inauguration of a president following his predecessor's death. William Cranch, chief judge of the United States Circuit Court for the District of Columbia, swore in both John Tyler, in 1841, and Millard Fillmore, in 1850.

There have been four other presidents who were sworn in by alternate judges: Chester A. Arthur, in 1881; Theodore Roosevelt, in 1901; Calvin Coolidge, in 1923; and Lyndon B. Johnson, in 1963. Each of these presidents was away from Washington when he learned that he was to become our nation's leader and, therefore, there was generally no choice other than to find the first available judge. In such instances, time was of the essence, for no one wanted our country to be without a president for any substantial period of time.

At George W. Bush's second inauguration, in 2005, there was some question as to whether Chief Justice William H. Rehnquist would be healthy enough to administer the oath. Three months earlier, Rehnquist had revealed that he was suffering from thyroid cancer. When he took his place on the podium just a few minutes before the ceremony, it was his first public appearance since that announcement. He walked very gingerly, aided by a cane, and wore a scarf to hide a tube that had been inserted into the front of his neck to help him breathe.

As Rehnquist slowly but clearly administered the oath to President Bush, spectators could hear a distinct, wheezing sound of air blowing through the tube. Bush called Rehnquist's appearance "an incredibly moving part of the ceremony." Chief Justice Rehnquist passed away just seven-and-a-half months after the 2005 Inauguration.

Different Strokes

Just as the words "so help me God" are not actually contained in the Constitution's section dealing with the president's inaugural oath, that document also sets forth no precise standards for exactly how the chief justice is to swear in a new president. Sometimes, the chief justice is on the left side of the inaugural platform, sometimes on the right side. Unlike the procession from the White House to the Capitol, during which the outgoing president traditionally sits on the right side of the vehicle, there is neither a rule nor a historical pattern to tell us which side of the platform the chief justice or the president will select when the oath is recited.

Even more significantly, the oath itself has been administered in different ways. Most ceremonies have featured the chief justice reciting the oath in portions, with the president then repeating those same phrases carefully and clearly, one part at a time.

For example, Chief Justice Rehnquist told President George W. Bush in 2005, "Please raise your right hand and repeat after me: I, George W. Bush, do solemnly swear...." Bush then said those same words. The two men alternately spoke the remaining parts of the oath, a few words at a time, and then concluded with "so help me God."

Chief Justice Earl Warren demonstrated a slightly different approach when he administered the oaths to four presidents—Eisenhower, Kennedy, Johnson, and Nixon—between 1957 and 1969. In 1961, for example, Warren said, "You, John Fitzgerald Kennedy, do solemnly swear...." The president would then respond, changing the word "you" to "I." This technique would continue throughout the oath, which was also recited in portions.

After Kennedy was assassinated in 1963, United States Federal District Judge Sarah T. Hughes was called upon to administer the oath to Lyndon B. Johnson. Hughes simply stated, "I do solemnly swear...." Johnson repeated her exact phrases. Neither Hughes nor Johnson ever mentioned the new president's name during that very sad inauguration in Dallas, Texas.

The procedure used for the oath in some earlier years was radically different. For example, when Chief Justice Edward D. White swore in Woodrow Wilson in 1913 and 1917, White recited the entire oath, without stopping, almost in the form of a question. When he was done, Wilson then only said two words: "I do." White swore in Warren G. Harding the same way in 1921, and Chief Justice William Howard Taft also followed this approach at the inaugurations of Calvin Coolidge and Herbert Hoover in 1925 and 1929.

In 1933, Chief Justice Charles Evans Hughes similarly recited the full oath without a stop. Franklin D. Roosevelt then repeated the entire oath, again without interruption, concluding with the words "so help me God."

Let's Hear It for the Girl

On March 1, 1929, three days before the upcoming inauguration, Chief Justice William Howard Taft wrote the following note to President-elect Herbert Hoover:

> I have thought it would be wise to put into written form the details of the ceremony of taking the oath, so that, subject to your approval, you and I shall know what we are to do.

> The ceremony will begin behind the stand where the oath is to be taken, you with your back to the Senate, and I with my back to the House. Without any preliminaries, I am to say:

> "You, Herbert Hoover, do solemnly swear that you will faithfully execute the office of President of the United States, and will to the best of your ability preserve, protect and defend the Constitution of the United States."

> You will then answer "I do."

Sure enough, three days later, as millions of Americans listened to a live radio broadcast of the ceremony, Taft recited the oath and Hoover said just those two words. Those listeners included an eighth-grade history class in Walden, New York. One of the students in that class was thirteen-year-old Helen Terwilliger. Helen had memorized the oath, and she was amazed to hear the chief justice conclude, "preserve, maintain, and defend the Constitution of the United States."

Chief Justice William Howard Taft, left, did most of the talking—and botched part of the oath—when he swore in Herbert Hoover as president in 1929. **Library of Congress,** Prints and Photographs Division, National Photo Company Collection, reproduction number LC-USZ62-17145.

Although no one else had noticed such an error, Helen was certain Taft had mistakenly substituted the word "maintain" for the word "protect." She was so sure, in fact, that she wrote a polite letter to the chief justice in Washington to tell him so.

Taft then wrote back to Helen, "You are quite right that the words of the oath mentioned in the Constitution are 'preserve, protect and defend,' but my memory is not always accurate and one sometimes becomes a little uncertain.… It certainly did not prevent the validity of the oath." But the seventy-one-year-old Taft also advised Helen, "You are mistaken in your report of what I did say. What I said was 'preserve, maintain and protect.' What I should have said was 'preserve, protect and defend,' and you may attribute the variation to the defect of an old man's memory."

Even after the young critic received this letter from Taft, she stood her ground. She insisted that her version of the chief justice's mistake reflected what had really taken place in Washington. To settle the issue, the Fox Film Corporation, Pathe News, and Paramount News all checked their inauguration sound films. On March 14, these three organizations unanimously declared that Helen had correctly quoted Taft's words. Not only had Taft misstated the oath; he had also been mistaken in his recollection of the particulars of his original error. Or, as the *New York World* reflected on Helen's accuracy: "She, not the Chief Justice, was right about the way in which the Chief Justice was wrong."

Upon learning the error of his ways, Chief Justice Taft later laughed and said, "I think you'll have to get along with what I've already said. After all, I don't think it's important."

When Americans went to movie theaters that week, they got to see and hear the sound newsreel of the ceremony. Then, absolutely everyone knew the truth: little Helen Terwilliger had been right all along.

The Bible, a Chair, and a Lock of Hair

The Bible that was used at George Washington's inauguration in 1789 has been preserved in the archives of the St. John's Masonic Lodge in New York City. Four other presidents, recognizing their historic link to that first ceremony, have arranged to have that very Bible transported to Washington so that they could place their hand upon it during their oaths. Those presidents were Warren G. Harding, in 1921; Dwight D. Eisenhower, in 1953; Jimmy Carter, in 1977; and George Bush, in 1989.

A few other presidents have also used similar links to the past in their inaugurations. Ulysses S. Grant, in 1873, and James A. Garfield, in 1881, each sat in the same chair that George Washington used during the 1789 ceremony. In 1905, John Hay, Theodore Roosevelt's secretary of state, sent the president a locket that included a lock of Abraham Lincoln's hair. Roosevelt was a great admirer of Lincoln, and Hay had been one of Lincoln's secretaries forty years earlier. Roosevelt was inspired by this gesture, and the president carried the locket with him while he was sworn in. And, speaking of links, George W. Bush was able to *wear* a link to the past. In 2001, Bush wore the same pair of cuff links that his father had worn at his own 1989 Inauguration.

A Bible has been a part of almost every inauguration, but records from 1825 indicate that John Quincy Adams used a book of constitutional law instead. Rutherford B. Hayes did not use a Bible at his private ceremony in 1877, but he did use one at the public celebration two days later. There were also three sudden inaugurations where no Bible or

A new tradition began at Lyndon B. Johnson's 1965 Inauguration when Lady Bird Johnson held the Bible during the inaugural oath. On the right is Chief Justice Earl Warren, and Vice President Hubert Humphrey is also in the picture. **Library of Congress,** Prints and Photographs Division, New York World Telegram and Sun Newspaper Photograph Collection, reproduction number LC-USZ62-120411.

other book was used at all. Chester A. Arthur was sworn in at his own home in 1881 following the death of James A. Garfield, but there was no Bible at the house. Similarly, when Theodore Roosevelt became president after William McKinley's assassination, in 1901, the oath was administered at a friend's home where no Bible could be found. In 1923, when Calvin Coolidge succeeded to the presidency upon the death of Warren G. Harding, a Bible was on the table in Coolidge's father's home, but it was not formally used.

Herbert Hoover kept his right hand on the Bible while the oath was recited in 1929, with his left hand always at his side. Then, in 1961, John F. Kennedy's left hand inadvertently slipped off the Bible as he was taking the oath, and most pictures from that swearing-in showed the new president's traditional right hand in the air, but his entire left arm straight by his side.

During an inauguration ceremony, anyone can be asked to have the honor of holding the Bible as the oath is administered to the new president. For many years, the clerk of the United States Supreme Court would hold the Bible. Such was the case, for example, in 1961 when Court Clerk James R. Browning held it at Kennedy's inauguration. At the very next formal inauguration, in 1965, President Lyndon B. Johnson asked his wife, Lady Bird, to hold the Bible as he was sworn in. Mrs. Johnson later wrote, "I was touched that Lyndon wanted me to hold the Bible for the swearing-in. We used the Bible Lyndon's mother had given us for Christmas in 1952, just after we moved to the ranch, and I stood facing the throng between the Chief Justice and Lyndon while he took the oath." This was the first time that a first lady had taken an active role in an inauguration. A precedent had been set, for the first lady has held the Bible at every inauguration since that one.

A Biblical Journey

In 2001, President-elect George W. Bush made arrangements to use the original George Washington Bible at his inauguration, as his father had twelve years earlier. The day before the ceremony, the master of the St. John's Masonic Lodge, Paul Magnotta, placed the famous Bible into a small, brown, leather satchel. Magnotta then boarded a New York train bound for Washington, traveling almost the same route—but in the opposite direction—that George Washington followed in his journey from his Mt. Vernon home to his New York City inauguration. Accompanied by two other lodge members, John Mountain and Jules Garfunkel, Magnotta brought the Bible to the Capitol the next morning.

The Bible was taken to a waiting area, the office of U.S. Senator Kay Bailey Hutchison of Texas. The weather outside was gloomy, with rain and sleet coming down. The inauguration committee prohibited the use of umbrellas at the ceremony. The committee also wanted everything in place on the podium by 10:00 a.m.—including the Bible.

At another cold and rainy inauguration, in 1937, a sheet of cellophane had been used to protect President Franklin D. Roosevelt's two-hundred-year-old family Bible. Roosevelt had then slipped his hand under the cellophane in order to place his hand upon the Bible during the oath.

But the St. John's Lodge members were not willing to allow the fragile George Washington Bible to sit in the open air for two hours before Bush's swearing-in at noon. They were only willing to have the Bible brought out at the last minute, in order to assure that it would not be damaged in any way.

The weather never improved, and the Bible remained in Senator Hutchison's office during the entire ceremony. George W. Bush used a family Bible instead. The St. John's members watched the inauguration on television from the senator's office, the book always by their side. The three men then returned the Bible to New York City the next day.

In and Out

B ecause of the historic nature of the first presidential inauguration, George Washington took his oath of office on an open balcony of New York's Federal Hall. A large crowd of people was outside, and they cheered wildly upon seeing the nation's first president sworn in. Washington then went back inside Federal Hall to give his inaugural address.

Inaugurations remained indoors until 1817. At that time, there was a temporary Capitol building called Congress Hall, commonly referred to as the "Brick Capitol," located where the U.S. Supreme Court is now situated. It was a structure that had been hastily built after the British set fire to most of Washington's public buildings during the War of 1812. In Congress Hall, the Senate was on the first floor and the House of Representatives occupied the second floor. Both bodies wanted to host the inaugural ceremonies in 1817. No one could agree, so President-elect James Monroe settled the issue: "Very well," he said, "I'll take my oath of office outdoors." He was sworn in on an elevated platform outside the Brick Capitol before the largest assembly of people to witness an inauguration up to that time.

Twelve years later, in 1829, the "People's President," Andrew Jackson, began the tradition of bringing the inauguration outside on a permanent basis. The Capitol had been restored, and a great throng of people gathered at the East Portico to witness the ceremony.

Chief Justice Warren E. Burger administered the oath to Ronald Reagan in the U.S. Capitol Rotunda in 1985, when freezing temperatures forced the ceremony to be moved indoors. **Office of the Sergeant at Arms, United States Senate.**

In 1833, because of his poor health, and also because of very cold weather, Jackson's second inauguration ceremony took place inside the House of Representatives chamber. Since then, every single president has scheduled both his oath and address to be outside so that as many people as possible could be a part of the occasion. But two other inauguration ceremonies—William Howard Taft's in 1909 and Ronald Reagan's in 1985—had to be moved indoors because of poor weather conditions. Taft's inauguration was moved into the Senate chamber. Reagan's was held inside the Capitol Rotunda and was viewed by approximately one thousand guests, rather than the one hundred and forty thousand who had tickets for the canceled ceremony at the Capitol's West Front.

An example of the symbolic importance of bringing the ceremony closer to the people occurred in 1913. Military security had cordoned off an area in front of the inaugural stand. President-elect Woodrow Wilson could see that there was thus a vacant area with a large contingent of people beyond the roped-off section, citizens who longed to be closer. "Let the people come forward!" Wilson proclaimed to security personnel. According to the *New York Times*, the people came forward "on a run and with a whoop. As they surged over the big open area, they cheered wildly and waived their hats." They were then able to better see and hear the ceremony, and they therefore felt more a part of it.

March to January

A study of the dates that our presidents served their posts leaves the immediate realization that most of them began and ended their terms on the date of March 4. Now, of course, our inauguration date is always January 20. In fact, all presidential inaugurations through 1933 were scheduled for March 4. Even George Washington's 1789 ceremony was supposed to be on that date; but, unfortunately, the Congress couldn't get enough of its members to show up to constitute a quorum in order to conduct business. As a result, Washington wasn't formally elected until April 6. "The delay is inauspicious to say the best of it," said Washington at the time. He was notified of his victory shortly thereafter, and the date of April 30, 1789, was then set as our country's first inauguration date.

Our nation's first legislative body, the Continental Congress, had originally set the first Wednesday in March to be the day that the president would be inaugurated in 1789. That first Wednesday happened to be on March 4. The same Congress decided to fix March 4 as the date for all future ceremonies. Part of the explanation at the time was that their study of future calendars had revealed that this choice of a date was one which was the least likely to cause Inauguration Day to fall on a Sunday, a day of the week on which the more religious politicians wished to avoid official business whenever possible.

An inauguration date in March always meant that the new president, after having been elected in November, would have to wait four months to actually assume his new office. This lengthy delay also affected members of the Senate and Congress. It meant that newly elected senators and representatives would be prevented from meeting and transacting business. The delay also allowed legislators who had been defeated in the November election to linger on in Washington, slipping some bills into law that only a person about to retire from public life would have considered sponsoring. Worse still, these "lame ducks" could block or filibuster to death other legislation that the people may have mandated through their recent election statement.

In the early days of our Republic, perhaps a delay of four months had been necessary, due to the available methods of transportation and communication at the time. But, by the time Congress had passed the Twentieth Amendment to the United States Constitution, in 1933, it was clear to all that four months was way too long to wait. During the debate on the proposed change, the Senate originally wanted January 15 while the House of Representatives suggested January 24. January 20 was reached as a compromise, and thus the amendment states:

> Section 1. The terms of the President and Vice President shall end at noon on the 20th of January ... and the terms of their successors shall then begin.

Franklin D. Roosevelt became the first president to be inaugurated on the new date, in 1937, thereby causing his first term to be forty-three days short of lasting four full years. The Senate and Congress now begin their terms on January 3. At that time, they are able to begin some of their work, as well as their preparations for the presidential inauguration. Thus, by necessity, there is still a "lame duck" period between November and January, but it is not nearly as long as it used to be.

East Side, West Side

The presidential inauguration is now always held on the terrace level of the West Front of the Capitol, allowing a majestic view of the Potomac River, Pennsylvania Avenue, the National Mall, the Washington Monument, and the Lincoln Memorial. This is a very new tradition, begun in 1981 at the first inauguration of Ronald Reagan. It allows for more people than ever before to view the festivities. The vast, open space on the west side makes it unlikely that the problems of 1809 or 1825 will ever arise again.

At James Madison's ceremony in 1809, an estimated ten thousand people had tried to push their way into the House of Representatives chamber amidst charges of graft in the distribution of tickets. Fistfights had broken out at the same location on John Quincy Adams's Inauguration Day, in 1825, again because there were not enough tickets and not enough room for everyone to view the events of the day.

Before 1981, all prior outdoor inaugurations had been on the east side of the Capitol, perhaps more residential in nature, but certainly not nearly as inspirational as the view from the west. From the Capitol's East Portico, one sees a very large area of a blacktop parking lot, commonly called the Capitol Plaza or East Plaza. Nearby are the Library of Congress and the United States Supreme Court, located on the spot where old Congress Hall used to be. It was right outside Congress Hall that James Monroe was inaugurated in the first outdoor ceremony in 1817. All other outdoor inaugurations between 1829 and 1977 were held on the steps in front of the

Most presidential inaugurations between 1829 and 1977 took place on the Capitol's East Portico. This picture is from Richard Nixon's 1973 swearing-in. **Architect of the Capitol.**

A different view of an inauguration on the East Portico. This 1949 picture shows the large crowd on the Capitol Plaza that was present for Harry S. Truman's ceremony. **Architect of the Capitol.**

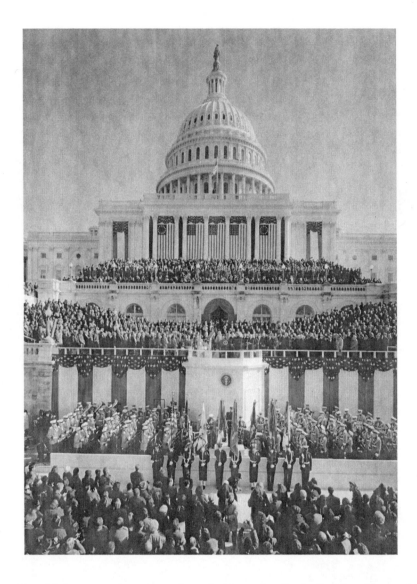

Presidential inaugurations have been held at the Capitol's West Front since 1981. This picture is from Bill Clinton's 1993 swearing-in. **Architect of the Capitol.**

Another view of a West Front inauguration. This picture is from Ronald Reagan's 1981 ceremony, the first one to take place on the Capitol's west side. The National Mall, including the Washington Monument, can be seen in the background. **Architect of the Capitol.**

Central Portico on the East Front of the Capitol. Most of the great history of inaugurations—including those of Lincoln, Roosevelt and Kennedy—occurred on those East Portico steps.

But prior to the 1981 event, Senator Mark Hatfield of Oregon, the chairman of the Joint Congressional Committee on Inaugural Ceremonies, suggested that it be moved to the west side, and President-elect Reagan agreed to the change. In his inaugural address that year, Reagan mentioned the new surroundings. "This is the first time in our history that this ceremony has been held on the West Front of the Capitol building," he said. "Standing here, we face a magnificent vista, opening up on this city's special beauty and history. At the end of this open mall are those shrines to the giants on whose shoulders we stand."

Never on Sunday

Our Inauguration Day has fallen on a Sunday on six occasions, but there has never been a public ceremony on that day of the week. The first time this occurred was in 1821. President James Monroe was to be sworn in for his second term in office, and upon the advice of United States Supreme Court Chief Justice John Marshall, Monroe's ceremony was postponed to Monday, March 5, 1821. Similarly, Zachary Taylor's inauguration took place on Monday, March 5, 1849.

The four other presidents whose Inauguration Day fell on a Sunday were actually sworn in twice. Rutherford B. Hayes was sworn in privately a day early, on March 3, 1877, as well as publicly on March 5 of that year.

Woodrow Wilson became the first person to be sworn in on a Sunday in 1917. With war already raging in Europe—a war that the United States would enter just a little over a month later—the Congress felt that our country should not be without a president for even one day. So, Wilson was sworn in privately in the president's office at the Capitol on Sunday, an event that lasted for less than one minute. The *New York Times* called the event "the most informal, casual, incidental inauguration ever held in our history." Wilson was administered the oath again publicly the very next day in a ceremony heavily guarded by soldiers on the streets and on rooftops, much like the inaugural scene at Lincoln's ceremony in 1861.

This new tradition of reciting the oath of office on two consecutive days continued with Dwight D. Eisenhower in 1957 and Ronald Reagan

Dwight D. Eisenhower's private ceremony in the East Room of the White House on Sunday, January 20, 1957. He was sworn in again publicly the next day. **Dwight D. Eisenhower Library,** U.S. Navy photograph.

in 1985, both of whom had private Sunday ceremonies at the White House.

Our Presidential Inauguration Day in 2013 will fall on a Sunday. Thus, we can once again anticipate a private Sunday ceremony, followed by the public celebration on Monday, January 21, 2013.

One-Day Wonders

On three of the six times that the normal Inauguration Day has fallen on a Sunday, the new president has taken the oath privately on the Sunday, and then again publicly on Monday. Those occurred in 1917, 1957 and 1985.

In 1877, President Hayes took the oath privately a full day early, on Saturday, and then again in public two days later. That was the only time in history when our elected president was sworn into office before the date prescribed by the U.S. Constitution.

The other two years when the inaugural date fell on a Sunday were 1821 and 1849. In those two years, President James Monroe and President Zachary Taylor did not have a private oath taking. Each simply postponed his ceremony until Monday, March 5.

But, according to the Constitution, Monroe's first term (and that of Vice President Daniel D. Tompkins) expired at noon on March 4, 1821. Similarly, the term of President James K. Polk (and Vice President George M. Dallas) expired at noon on March 4, 1849. Congress had passed a law in 1792 saying that, if those offices were vacant, the responsibilities of the chief executive would pass to the president pro tempore of the United States Senate.

In 1821, the president pro tempore of the Senate was Senator John Gaillard of South Carolina. Because March 4, 1821, fell on a Sunday, one could say that Gaillard served as president of the United States for one day—right in the middle of Monroe's two four-year terms!

A similar situation arose in 1849, and some historians believe that Senator David Rice Atchison of Missouri was also president for a day on Sunday, March 4, 1849. He had been president pro tempore of the Senate through Saturday, March 3; but, in his case, his term ran out on Saturday, and he was technically out of office until his new term as senator began again on Monday. So, our country may have actually had no legal president from noon on March 4, 1849, until noon the next day, when President Taylor was sworn in.

Nevertheless, written on Atchison's tombstone in Missouri are the words, "David Rice Atchison, 1807–1886, President of the U.S. one day."

And, when Atchison was later asked what he did on his one day as our nation's leader, he said, "I went to bed. There had been two or three big nights finishing up the work of the Senate, and I slept most of that Sunday."

Sneaking into Town

The contestants for president in 1876 were Republican Rutherford B. Hayes and Democrat Samuel J. Tilden. Tilden received about two hundred fifty thousand more popular votes than Hayes, but it was Hayes who won by just one vote in the Electoral College. The final outcome wasn't revealed until March 2, 1877, just three days before the inauguration, when a special commission gave twenty disputed electoral votes to Hayes. Many citizens in the country felt that the Republicans had stolen the election. Some people began calling Hayes "His Fraudulency."

The normal day for the upcoming inauguration, March 4, fell on a Sunday in 1877. Following the precedents set in 1821 and 1849, the plan was to have the ceremony take place on Monday, March 5.

But rumors began to fly that Tilden would have himself sworn in on March 4 and declare himself the real president. So, an extraordinary event took place. The outgoing president, Ulysses S. Grant, invited Hayes to the White House for dinner on Saturday night, March 3. Grant had experienced the horrors of the Civil War and didn't want to see the country head into another disaster, so he helped arrange for Hayes to be sworn into office that night! Chief Justice Morrison R. Waite administered the oath to Hayes in the Red Room of the White House, thereby making Hayes the only person to ever be sworn in prior to the official Inauguration Day. It also meant that the United States technically had two presidents at the same time.

Sunday, March 4, passed without incident, and then Hayes was sworn in again on Monday in a public ceremony at the Capitol.

Streaking into Town

As Chief Justice William H. Rehnquist began to administer the oath of office to George W. Bush, in 2001, many inauguration spectators began snapping photos. But in a few sections near the inaugural platform, they weren't photographing the ceremony itself. Instead, their attention had been drawn to Joan Roney and Matthew Power, two spectators who had suddenly disrobed and were now walking up and down the aisles.

Inauguration ticket holders are prohibited from displaying any signs, placards or stickers. But because Roney and Power wished to protest at Bush's inauguration, they painted their bodies. Power had the words "No Mandate" on him, referring to Bush's disputed election victory. On Roney's chest were the words "No Democracy?" with the question mark right on her navel. Her back read "Hail to the Thief." She also had "One Person, One Vote" on her right arm, and "Ricky Martin, how could you?" on her left arm—indicating her sadness that a well-known singer was performing at one of the inaugural events.

As Roney and Power walked the aisles, Republican Party guests yelled at them, "Hope you catch pneumonia," "Hope you freeze to death," and "Go back to Arkansas"—a reference to outgoing President Bill Clinton. The two protesters were detained by the police and Secret Service and held at the police station for an hour and a half before being released.

That protest marked the first time an inaugural oath had been disrupted. Four years later, George W. Bush also became the first president to have his inaugural address disrupted. While Bush was delivering his speech, six members of the women's peace activist group Code Pink stood on their chairs and shouted, "Bring the troops home now," "End the celebration, stop the occupation," and "Champagne is flying while soldiers are dying"—all in response to the United States' war in Iraq.

Many Bush supporters then attempted to drown out the women by yelling "Four more years." When the police tried to get everyone to settle down, Code Pink cofounder Jodie Evans responded by saying, "The freedom to speak is being exercised. Bush is talking about freedom."

After a number of minutes, spectators forced the protesters down from atop the chairs. The police pulled the Code Pink members' arms and wrists behind them and escorted the six women away from the ceremony area. Evans later called the episode "a memorable occasion ... and very painful."

Super Bowl Connection

O ur Presidential Inauguration Day always takes place in late January. One of the biggest days in sports, the National Football League's annual Super Bowl, is always played around the same time of the year.

The inauguration is held in Washington, D.C., before a great gathering of people outside our nation's Capitol. Millions more watch the event on television. The Super Bowl shifts among various cities and is always played before a sellout stadium crowd. Millions more view the game on television every year, and many people have parties in their homes to watch the game with friends.

The 2009 Inauguration, on January 20, is formally called the Fifty-sixth Presidential Inauguration. The forty-third Super Bowl is in Tampa, Florida, just twelve days later, on February 1, and it is officially titled Super Bowl XLIII.

Because inaugurations take place only once every four years, and because the Super Bowl is played every single year, it won't be that long before there will have been more Super Bowls than presidential inaugurations. The year 2025 will mark the sixtieth inauguration and the fifty-ninth Super Bowl. So, by the year 2027, there will have been more Super Bowls than formal inaugurations, even though the first inauguration was in 1789 and the first Super Bowl didn't take place until 1967.

One year, the inauguration and the Super Bowl virtually came together as one. The San Francisco 49ers played the Miami Dolphins in Super Bowl

XIX on January 20, 1985, the same exact day as the private ceremony for President Ronald Reagan's second inauguration. Because January 20 fell on a Sunday that year, Reagan's public ceremony was planned for Monday, January 21. But, in addition to his private taking of the oath at the White House that Sunday, President Reagan also played a role in the traditional coin toss to start the football game.

The captains of the 49ers met their counterparts for the Dolphins at the center of the field. With a television camera in the White House, the image of the president flipping the coin was then beamed across the country to the Diamond Vision screen at Stanford Stadium in Palo Alto, California. Miami Captain Dwight Stephenson called heads. "It is tails," said Reagan, who then told the players and the crowd, "May everyone do their best, may there be no injuries, may the best team win, may no one have regrets." The 49ers had won the toss, and they would go on to win the game by a score of 38-16. Reagan watched the contest from the White House, and then he was sworn in again the next day.

I've Seen Fire

Richard Cardinal Cushing was just beginning to deliver the invocation at President John F. Kennedy's 1961 Inauguration. Spectators, as well as a national television audience, suddenly began to notice smoke coming from the area of the speaker's lectern. It appeared that the wooden inaugural platform might be on fire.

Secret Service agents and electricians quickly worked to locate the problem. The Secret Service blamed the problem on a smoldering wire in a heater that had been placed inside the lectern to help keep the speakers warm. The electricians believed that the problem was really a short circuit in the electric motor used to raise and lower the lectern according to the individual speaker's height.

Whatever the cause, the problem ended as soon as the electrical appliances were disconnected. Meanwhile, Cardinal Cushing had continued on with his invocation without a pause.

... and I've Seen Rain

With our Inauguration Day always taking place in January, and prior to 1937 in early March, it should not be surprising to know that bad weather has sometimes been a bit of a problem. James Monroe had enjoyed Washington's first outdoor inauguration, in 1817, and had hoped to have another outdoor ceremony at his second inauguration four years later, but poor weather moved the festivities into the House of Representatives. The same thing occurred with Andrew Jackson's second ceremony, in 1833. William Howard Taft's 1909 Inauguration was moved indoors into the Senate chamber due to a storm that dropped nearly ten inches of snow over the Washington area, causing Taft to quip, "I always said it would be a cold day when I got to be president of the United States." The last inauguration to be moved indoors was Ronald Reagan's second ceremony, in 1985. It was transferred to the Capitol Rotunda because of bitterly cold weather.

One president who undoubtedly should have moved his inauguration indoors was William Henry Harrison, in 1841. On another freezing and windy day, Harrison extended himself too much, riding on horseback, delivering an overly long speech, and partying deep into the night. He caught pneumonia and died after only a month in office.

It was a cold, snowy, and windy day in 1893 when Grover Cleveland was inaugurated for the second time. The wind blew the hats off a number of dignitaries, causing laughter among the crowd below the stage. When Cleveland voluntarily took his hat off before addressing the throng, many spectators were concerned that he should not be bareheaded in the twenty-five-degree temperature and shouted to him, "Put on your hat!" Cleveland braved the cold weather, delivering his speech without his hat.

Theodore Roosevelt also experienced a very windy day in 1905. During his inaugural address, the wind blew the cord of his eyeglasses all around his face. It even blew into his mouth at one point, interrupting his speech.

Some of the hardest rain at an inauguration took place in 1845 when, according to John Quincy Adams, the new president, James K. Polk, "delivered his address to a large assemblage of umbrellas." Then, in 1889, during another violent rainstorm, outgoing President Grover Cleveland held an umbrella over the head of successor Benjamin Harrison during the ceremonies at the Capitol. The *New York Times* described the scene as "an unbroken line of umbrellas. One would scarcely have believed there were so many umbrellas in Washington."

Parades were canceled because of cold weather in 1833 and 1985. Pennsylvania Avenue was a sea of mud in 1865, and the weather was cold enough to affect guests at the inaugural ball in 1873, even though the ball was indoors. For the record, the coldest inauguration was in 1985 when the temperature reached a high of just seven degrees (with a windchill factor of minus twenty-two degrees), while the warmest temperature ever for a traditional inauguration in Washington has been fifty-five degrees, in both 1913 and 1981. Thus, Ronald Reagan has the unique distinction of having been inaugurated on both the warmest and coldest days.

In 1937, the official day for the ceremony changed from March 4 to January 20. The weather for Franklin D. Roosevelt's ceremony that year was terrible. There was a new Washington rainfall record of 1.77 inches for the date of January 20, and the temperature at noon was just thirty-

There were lots of umbrellas among the crowd that witnessed Benjamin Harrison's inauguration in 1889. **Library of Congress,** Prints and Photographs Division, reproduction number LC-USZ62-63418.

In 1909, President Theodore Roosevelt and President-elect William Howard Taft rode together to the Capitol, in a closed carriage, when a huge snowstorm hit Washington. **Library of Congress,** Prints and Photographs Division, George Grantham Bain Collection, reproduction number LC-USZ62-32737.

two degrees. As luck would have it, the weather on March 4 that year was sixty-seven degrees and sunny.

Finally, at one inauguration, it was the sun that caused a problem! Prior to John F. Kennedy's 1961 Inauguration, eighty-six-year-old poet Robert Frost had written a poem for the occasion called "Dedication." It had snowed the night before the ceremony, but now the sun was shining brightly and the sky was blue. Frost was about to begin to read his poem, but the very bright glare of the snow prevented him from being able to see what he had written. Even new Vice President Lyndon Johnson's efforts to create some shade for Frost, with a top hat, didn't help. Frost could be heard to say, "I'm not having a good light" and "I can't see in the sun." So, instead, Frost delivered an older poem, "The Gift Outright," one that he had memorized.

But even then, Frost's problems didn't end. He concluded his presentation by informing the assembled throng that his poetry had been dedicated "to the president-elect, Mr. John Finley." Frost had inadvertently stated the name of a scholar from Harvard. Finley knew Frost. Finley may have been a friend of Frost. But Finley was no Jack Kennedy.

Eight Is Not Enough

Until 1940, no person had ever been elected to serve three terms as president. George Washington had set a precedent when he decided that eight years as our nation's chief executive were enough. The only person who had even tried to get elected for a third time was Theodore Roosevelt, in 1912.

But in 1940, the people of our country did not want a new president. Franklin Roosevelt had led them out from the depths of the Great Depression, and with war already raging in Europe, the time had come to elect a president for a third time. Roosevelt would lead us through most of World War II and be re-elected for a fourth term in 1944.

Because of the war, Roosevelt's inauguration on January 20, 1945 was a quiet one. It took place at the South Portico of the White House, rather than on the Capitol steps. There was no parade and no ball. The inauguration lunch consisted of cold chicken salad and pound cake. Less than three months later, Roosevelt died. He had been president for twelve years, one month, and eight days, longer than anyone else in history.

In 1951, Congress passed the Twenty-second Amendment to the United States Constitution. That amendment begins with the words, "No person shall be elected to the office of President more than twice …"

That amendment also states that one can also serve two fully elected terms if he or she has served no more than two years of the previous president's term. So, for example, when Lyndon B. Johnson served out

Franklin D. Roosevelt's fourth inauguration, in 1945, took place on a White House balcony, rather than at the Capitol. The crowd stood in the snow during that quiet ceremony. **Library of Congress,** Prints and Photographs Division, Harris and Ewing Collection, reproduction number LC-H212-C-1983.

the final year and two months of President Kennedy's term, he was still eligible to serve eight more years as president. After being elected in his own right in 1964, however, President Johnson chose not to run again in 1968.

Under this amendment, no one will ever again serve as president as long as Franklin Roosevelt.

We Are Family

Three of the most touching moments at a presidential inauguration took place at Ulysses S. Grant's first ceremony, in 1869; James A. Garfield's big day in 1881; and George W. Bush's inauguration in 2001. Grant had just begun his inaugural address when, suddenly, his fourteen-year-old daughter, Nellie, ran forward to him. She grasped her father's hand as he continued to speak to the crowd. Someone brought over a chair for her, and Nellie sat down next to her father for the duration of the address. Later in the day, during the inaugural parade, some marching troops passed by the new first family and shouted out, "Three cheers for our Nellie!"

Garfield's inauguration in 1881 represented the very first time that a president's mother was present to see the swearing-in of her son. That year was also the first ceremony in which the first lady—as well as the new president's mother—was allowed to sit in the front row, next to the railing on the inaugural platform. Women had previously been required to sit in the rear rows on the platform. After delivering his inaugural address and taking the oath of office, Garfield's very first act as president was to give his mother a kiss. A contemporary publication called *Frank Leslie's Illustrated Newspaper* commented on Garfield's gesture, reporting that "nobody could see it without being deeply touched, and the incident went straight to the hearts of the people."

In 2001, George W. Bush joined John Quincy Adams as the only sons of former presidents to later be elected to the same high office. When

Adams was inaugurated in 1825, his mother, Abigail, had already passed away, and his father, John, was living in Massachusetts and was too ill to attend the ceremony. But both of George W. Bush's parents, George and Barbara, attended the 2001 and 2005 Inaugurations. In the days leading up to the first ceremony, both father and son often mentioned the deep emotions they were feeling. The first President Bush said, "I hope if tears flow, people understand that they are looking at the proudest father in the USA."

When President-elect Bush exited the Capitol and walked down a set of stairs and onto the inaugural platform, he shook hands with the many dignitaries present for the event; but he did not acknowledge his parents. After taking the oath of office, he then shook hands with the outgoing president, Bill Clinton, the outgoing vice president, Al Gore, and the new vice president, Dick Cheney. He then turned to his parents. He hugged his dad and kissed his mom. As the new president returned to his seat, his father wiped away a tear.

Talking the Talk

Although the inaugural address is usually both a very eagerly antici-
pated event and one that is later analyzed ad nauseum by members
of the press, the true historic reality is that most inauguration speeches
have been eminently forgettable. Many of them have been filled with
generalities about faith and prayer, doing good deeds, and getting along
with one another—words that could have been said in the eighteenth
century as well as the twenty-first.

Yet, such themes are generally appropriate to the occasion. After an election that has ended only recently, a new president would certainly want
to try to unify the people. In 1913, Woodrow Wilson told the spectators,
"This is not a day of triumph; it is a day of dedication. Here muster not
the forces of party but the forces of humanity." George Bush's words in
1989 were, "This is a day when our nation is made whole, when our differences, for a moment, are suspended."

Similarly, John F. Kennedy began his 1961 inaugural address by saying,
"We observe today not a victory of party but a celebration of freedom—
symbolizing an end as well as a beginning—signifying renewal as well
as change. For I have sworn before you and Almighty God the same solemn oath our forebears prescribed nearly a century and three-quarters
ago." In 1993, Bill Clinton also used the word "renewal" in his speech,
calling for "a new season of American renewal."

71

The inaugural address is now always after the oath, as it was in 1789 with George Washington; but this has not always been the case. In fact, during most inaugurations in our nation's first one hundred years, the speech came first. For example, both of Abraham Lincoln's speeches came before the administration of the oath. But since the late 1800s, the oath has almost always preceded the address.

There are other common themes that seem to arise in virtually every inaugural address. The new president is likely to thank his predecessor for a job well done and express confidence that the American people have the will to do what is needed to improve our present situation. "We can do it if we work together," the new president is likely to say. Some, like Woodrow Wilson in 1917, will point out that we are "citizens of the world" and that our country shall continue to play a major role in events around the world.

The theme of an inaugural address often reflects the times. In 1881, James A. Garfield referred to African Americans who had recently attained citizenship after the Civil War. The next day's *New York Times* reported that Garfield's address was "remarkably effective, so much so that in many instances old black men, who had been slaves, were seen weeping in the crowd." In 1929, Herbert Hoover spoke about the need for prohibition laws to be enforced.

Some presidents may try to make predictions during the course of the speech. In 1873, Ulysses S. Grant stated his belief that the world would come together as one: "I believe that our Great Maker is preparing the world, in his own good time, to become one nation, speaking one language, and when armies and navies will no longer be required."

Yes, it's probably unlikely that an inaugural address will produce a speech for the ages. The speech might even be delivered "in a very low voice, and very badly, as to pronunciation and manner," as President James K. Polk critiqued the oratory of his successor, Zachary Taylor, in 1849. But four presidents–Thomas Jefferson, Abraham Lincoln, Franklin D. Roosevelt and John F. Kennedy–did deliver speeches that shall long endure, inaugural addresses that resonated with deep meaning and impassioned eloquence.

The First Change of Power

Between 1797 and 1801, Federalist Party member John Adams was our president. His vice president during that four-year period was Thomas Jefferson, a member of the main rival party at that time, the Democratic-Republicans. This unusual situation was the result of different laws in effect at the time, laws that called for the person who received the most electoral votes in our national election to be the president and the person having the second highest number of votes being deemed vice president, regardless of political affiliation. The Twelfth Amendment to the United States Constitution would change this procedure in 1804, allowing electors to vote separately for president and vice president.

Adams and Jefferson were bitter rivals. The Federalists had run our country during its formative years, and they had helped solve our early financial problems. Their methods appealed largely to people of wealth. Jefferson's followers were more middle class, such as farmers and workers in small businesses. Most Federalists believed that the Democratic-Republicans would weaken our military forces.

When Jefferson defeated Adams in the next election, there was major concern that the first transition of political power in our nation's history might result in turmoil and violence. President Adams wanted nothing to do with Jefferson's Inauguration Day on March 4, 1801. Adams left town because he felt that appearing at Jefferson's ceremony was as absurd a thought as the idea of King George III of England appearing at George Washington's inauguration in 1789.

Jefferson wanted his inauguration to be simple. On his big day, he walked from his boarding house to the Capitol with a few friends. He wore a casual suit, one that he had worn many times before. This was to be the first inauguration to ever take place in the new capital city of Washington, and everyone was anxious to hear what Jefferson would say.

His speech helped heal a nation. He spoke of reconciliation and of unity. He urged everyone to "unite in common efforts for the common good" and to "unite with one heart and one mind." Yes, Jefferson had just won the election. But he also showed that he cared about the vanquished when he discussed what he called a "sacred principle." Jefferson said, "[T]hough the will of the majority is in all cases to prevail, that will, to be rightful, must be reasonable; that the minority possess their equal rights, which equal laws must protect, and to violate which would be oppression."

But the true spirit of Jefferson's hopes came forth in these words: "We have called by different names brethren of the same principle. We are all Republicans, we are all Federalists."

The people of Washington were able to read the words of Jefferson's unifying oration within minutes of its conclusion. Earlier in the day, Jefferson had given an advance copy of his speech to his friend Samuel Harrison Smith, editor of *The National Intelligencer.* The speech was quickly printed in its entirety, the first "extra" edition of a newspaper in U.S. history.

The first transfer of power in our nation from one political party to another was a peaceful one. There was no bloodshed, no second American revolution, as some Federalists had feared. The tone had been set for all future orderly changes.

The Civil War Inaugurals

There were clouds of war over Washington on the day that Abraham Lincoln was inaugurated as our president on March 4, 1861. Soldiers were all along Pennsylvania Avenue and riflemen were on the rooftops, all guarding against potential assault on the carriage carrying the new president.

At the East Portico of the Capitol, Lincoln took off his top hat as he prepared to deliver his inaugural address. He stood awkwardly for a few moments, as he was not sure what to do with the hat. Stephen A. Douglas, the man whom Lincoln had defeated in the previous November's election, then stepped forward and offered to hold Lincoln's hat for him. Douglas said, "If I cannot be the president, I can at least hold his hat." This was not the first inauguration where Lincoln had problems with his hat. In 1849, he had been one of many guests at Zachary Taylor's inaugural ball who had lost a hat amidst the chaos of an unorganized party.

But it was the Union that was his only concern now. Until the moment that civil war would become a reality, Lincoln would try to do whatever he could to try to keep the republic together. "We are not enemies, but friends," he said in his address. "We must not be enemies." He told the crowd, "In your hands, my dissatisfied fellow countrymen, and not in mine, is the momentous issue of civil war.... You have no oath registered in heaven to destroy the government, while I have the most solemn one to 'preserve, protect and defend' it."

Abraham Lincoln, in center of picture, delivering his famous "with malice toward none, with charity for all" inaugural address in 1865. **Architect of the Capitol.**

Lincoln's appeal for harmony was eloquent, but the War Between the States was inevitable. The Civil War would begin just five and half weeks after the inauguration, and it would continue throughout almost his entire presidency. Lincoln had been sworn in under the shadow of an unfinished cast-iron Capitol dome, the old wooden one having been removed in 1855. As the Civil War raged on, work on the new dome continued, symbolic of the reality that our country's development and growth would proceed as well. When Lincoln was inaugurated for the beginning of his abbreviated second term, in 1865, the dome had been completed. The Union's victory in the war was at hand.

Lincoln's words that day were as gracious as they were memorable. He wanted both the victors and the vanquished to know that we were still one nation. "With malice toward none, with charity for all," he said, "with firmness in the right as God gives us to see the right, let us strive on to finish the work we are in, to bind up the nation's wounds, to care for him who shall have borne the battle for his widow and his orphan, to do all which may achieve and cherish a just and lasting peace among ourselves and all nations."

As these concluding words to his speech were pronounced, many people in the crowd were moved to tears.

A little over a month later, the Civil War came to its conclusion when Gen. Robert E. Lee surrendered to Gen. Ulysses S. Grant. President Lincoln would not be able to lead our country to the reunification that he had so much desired, however, for he was assassinated less than a week after the war ended.

Quelling Our Fears

"I am certain that my fellow Americans expect that on my induction into the Presidency I will address them with a candor and a decision which the present situation of our nation impels."

Those were the bold opening words of President Franklin D. Roosevelt's inaugural address on March 4, 1933. Our country was in the middle of the worst economic depression we had ever faced. Many citizens had lost their jobs. Farmers had lost their farms. Life savings had been wiped out when banks failed.

The people needed hope, and Roosevelt gave it to them when he said, "This great nation will endure as it has endured, will revive and will prosper. So, first of all, let me first assert my firm belief that the only thing we have to fear is fear itself—nameless, unreasoning, unjustified terror which paralyzes needed efforts to convert retreat into advance. In every dark hour of our national life a leadership of frankness and vigor has met with that understanding and support of the people themselves which is essential to victory. I am convinced that you will again give that support to leadership in these crucial days."

But as important as the need for hope, Roosevelt also asserted, "The nation asks for action and action now. We must act and act quickly.... Our greatest primary task is to put people to work." His call for action was met by Congress, which designed new laws to help the people in need. The Agricultural Adjustment Act aided the farmers. The Federal

Deposit Insurance Corporation was established to prevent any further banking crises. The Works Progress Administration helped create many jobs. The Social Security Act provided relief for the unemployed and insurance for our elderly citizens.

Roosevelt's inaugural address was met by quiet applause during much of the speech; but at the end, the cheers were roars of approval. Historian Arthur M. Schlesinger wrote that the speech "seemed to give the people, as well as myself, a new hold upon life."

The next day's *Washington Post* described the Inauguration Day crowd as one that "cheered with a confidence that had been strangely missing these last few months. Here, they seemed to say, was a man to lead them out of the wilderness of depression." Hope had indeed been generated, and action was about to begin. Roosevelt would lead our country out of the depression and would go on to serve as president longer than any person in history.

Inspiring a Generation

John F. Kennedy became the youngest man ever elected president of the United States. He was just forty-three when he was sworn into office on January 20, 1961. His predecessor, Dwight D. Eisenhower, had turned seventy before leaving office, so there was a clear change in power, not only from Republican to Democratic, but also from an older generation to a much younger one.

"Let the word go forth," Kennedy said, "… that the torch has been passed to a new generation of Americans—born in this century, tempered by war, disciplined by a hard and bitter peace, proud of our ancient heritage—and unwilling to witness or permit the slow undoing of those human rights to which this nation has always been committed." He asked the world community "to begin anew the quest for peace" and added these strong words: "Let every nation know, whether it wishes us well or ill, that we shall pay any price, bear any burden, meet any hardship, support any friend, oppose any foe to assure the survival and success of liberty."

At the time of his inauguration, the main adversary of the United States was the Soviet Union and its Communist block. Kennedy urged both sides to openly communicate with one another, adding in a firm voice, "Let us never negotiate out of fear. But let us never fear to negotiate."

Kennedy demonstrated that he had no such fears when he proclaimed, "In the long history of the world, only a few generations have been

John F. Kennedy being sworn in by Chief Justice Earl Warren in 1961, shortly before his memorable inaugural address. **National Archives and Records Administration,** Still Picture Reference Team, number 111-SC-578830.

granted the role of defending freedom in its hour of maximum danger. I do not shrink from this responsibility—I welcome it." He then expressed his strong belief that other Americans would join him in his efforts. "The energy, the faith, the devotion which we bring to this endeavor will light our country and all who serve it—and the glow from that fire can truly light the world.

"And so, my fellow Americans," Kennedy said, his voice rising, "ask not what your country can do for you—ask what you can do for your country."

Kennedy's dramatic inaugural address was interrupted numerous times by loud applause and cheering. The next day's *Washington Post* called the speech "surely one of the most eloquent in history."

Speechless in Washington

The president's inaugural address is always one of the highlights of the day. The vice president, on the other hand, doesn't do much more than take the oath of office. This event always takes place minutes before the president's oath and inaugural address.

The vice president now takes the oath outside on the Capitol steps, but it was not until 1937 that this procedure was followed for the first time. Prior to that year, the vice president would take his oath of office inside the Senate chamber, completely separate from the president's ceremony. Since the vice president's main function is that of president of the Senate, it was previously considered appropriate that his ceremony take place in that room.

The vice president also used to deliver an inaugural address of his own in front of the Senate. Some of these speeches were long, while others said little other than to invite the Senate members to now gather outside for the presidential swearing-in. The last vice president to deliver a speech at his inauguration was John Nance Garner in 1933; he spoke extemporaneously for only a couple of minutes. That year, as in previous years, the president entered the Senate chamber and watched the vice-presidential ceremony prior to everyone moving outside for the presidential inauguration.

One year, the vice president wasn't even in the country for his big day. In 1852, Franklin Pierce and William R. King had been elected president and vice president. The long campaign took its toll on King, and he became very ill. In early 1853, he went to Havana, Cuba, to try to recuperate.

King was still in Cuba on Inauguration Day, March 4, 1853. Through a special act of Congress, he was allowed to take his oath of office there, administered to him by the American consul in Cuba, and he returned to the United States shortly thereafter. But, sadly, King died on April 18, 1853 in his home state of Alabama, just six weeks after taking office.

In 1925, Vice President Charles G. Dawes delivered a loud and forceful vice-presidential address in which he condemned the Senate for wasting time in its operations. Dawes knew something about writing, as he had even penned a popular song called "It's All in the Game." But, when he gave his speech, the audience began to laugh at his mannerisms. The next day's *New York Times* reported that Dawes "waved his arms, he pounded the desk in front of him with loud, resounding thumps and he shook an admonitory finger toward the section where the senators were seated. His voice, a little husky, rang out. At times he shouted. Obviously, he intended to be emphatic. He furnished the sensation of the day."

Yet, perhaps the most famous—or infamous—vice-presidential speech was given by Andrew Johnson in 1865. Before the ceremony, Johnson had ingested some alcohol, supposedly to make him feel a bit better after having had a bout with typhoid fever. But when he began to speak, it was obvious to everyone that he was drunk. He rambled on incoherently and nearly passed out, causing all in the audience to turn, twist, and cover their faces in embarrassment. Senator Charles Sumner of Massachusetts called Johnson's speech "the most unfortunate thing that has occurred in our history."

Even President Abraham Lincoln was humiliated by Johnson's performance. When the vice president's speech was finally over, Lincoln told a marshal, "Do not let Johnson speak outside." And now, on Inauguration Day, except for taking of the oath itself, the vice president does not speak at all.

The Long and Short of It

The shortest inaugural address was delivered by President George Washington at his second inauguration, in 1793. His address consisted of just 135 words, saying simply that his administration would continue on as before. This speech was given indoors, inside the Senate chamber at Philadelphia's Congress Hall. Washington would go on to fully serve out his second term as president.

On the other side of the spectrum, the longest speech took place in 1841. William Henry Harrison spoke for two full hours—8,495 words that went on and on and on. This inaugural address, written by Daniel Webster, was delivered on a cold and blustery day. Harrison spoke without much in the way of wraps and without a hat on his head.

Harrison was sixty-eight, at that time the oldest man to ever become president. On his Inauguration Day, one might say that he did not consider his limitations. Aside from speaking too long, he also rode to the ceremony on his horse, turning down an invitation to travel by closed carriage. He then partied long into the night, at three separate inaugural balls. All of this activity proved too much for Harrison. He caught pneumonia and never recovered. He died on April 4, 1841, just one month after becoming president. No person has ever served as president for a shorter period of time.

For the record, Theodore Roosevelt delivered the second-shortest inaugural address, 985 words in 1905. James K. Polk made the second-longest speech, 4,776 words in 1845.

The Inauguration Wasn't
the Lead Story

For the final fourteen months of the administration of Jimmy Carter, and leading right up to the inauguration of Ronald Reagan in 1981, the United States had been involved in an international crisis involving Iran. A new government in that country was anti-American because the United States had supported the previous ruler, the Shah, and because our country had allowed the Shah to come here for medical treatment.

The new Iranian revolutionaries took a group of Americans—mostly workers at the American Embassy—as hostages. Negotiations on returning the hostages back to the United States preoccupied Jimmy Carter's final year in the White House.

Freedom finally came for the hostages on Reagan's Inauguration Day, January 20, 1981. While Carter and Reagan were having morning tea at the White House that day, they were advised that buses carrying the hostages were near the airport in Tehran. As Carter and Reagan entered the limousine to drive to the Capitol for the inaugural ceremonies, they learned that the fifty-two hostages were about to board planes that would be leaving Iran.

A few minutes later, while Carter and Reagan were traveling along Pennsylvania Avenue on their way to Capitol Hill, the news was that the airplanes would be departing imminently.

The inauguration ceremonies began at the West Front. Five minutes after President Reagan concluded his inaugural address, the hostages were flown out of Iran. The ceremony ended, and Congressional leaders hosted a Capitol luncheon in Reagan's honor at Statuary Hall. There, Reagan notified Congress and the television audience that the hostages had cleared Iranian airspace. He raised a glass of wine and said, "We can all drink to this one." Shortly thereafter, Reagan chose the outgoing president, Jimmy Carter, to fly to Europe to greet the released hostages on behalf of our country.

III

The Inaugural Parade

Everyone Loves a Parade!

The oath and inaugural address now complete, the ceremony has ended with the delivery of the benediction and the playing of our national anthem. The new president and his family will proceed to have lunch, usually inside the Capitol. At the George W. Bush 2005 Inauguration, here was the menu for the luncheon inside the Capitol's Statuary Hall:

Scalloped Crab and Lobster

Roasted Missouri Quail with Chestnuts and Brined Root Vegetables

Steamed Lemon Pudding

Apple Wild Cherry Compote

Then, after about an hour, it is time for the inaugural parade. The president and first lady lead off the parade, riding or walking together down Pennsylvania Avenue toward the White House. That famous street is lined with people, waving small American flags and cheering. All around the area, vendors are selling inaugural souvenirs: buttons, pins, pennants, programs, medallions, ashtrays, T-shirts, glasses, and coffee mugs.

When the president and spouse reach the area of the White House, they will then go to a reviewing stand that has been built in front of their new residence along Pennsylvania Avenue. That's where they'll relax and watch the rest of the parade. The first such reviewing stand was erected for James Garfield's inaugural parade in 1881. The reviewing stand is now likely to have bulletproof glass around it, a sad reminder of security that has been deemed necessary since the 1963 assassination of President Kennedy. But no one is in the mood to think about that now, because the parade is really just beginning.

The longest parade took place following President Dwight D. Eisenhower's inauguration in 1953: four hours and thirty-nine minutes. At that parade, Eisenhower even allowed himself to be lassoed by a cowboy named Monte Montana, much to the chagrin of the Secret Service, which had not been alerted to the prank.

The parade is likely to be more streamlined now, probably lasting a couple of hours, but still a far cry from the small, unplanned outbursts of emotion that followed George Washington's inauguration in 1789 and Thomas Jefferson's in 1805.

The president will applaud and wave to the parade participants who march past the reviewing stand. There will be many marching bands playing patriotic music. Members of the various armed services will pass by in military precision, ordered to take twenty-eight-inch steps to the beat of 110 steps per minute. Forty years before his own inauguration, Eisenhower was one of the West Point cadets who marched at Woodrow Wilson's 1913 inaugural parade.

There will be lots of horses, and maybe some elephants or donkeys. College and high school bands, drum corps, and baton twirlers will be on parade. Dance teams, choirs, and tumblers will have a chance to show off their stuff. There will also be plenty of colorful floats—not necessarily with patriotic themes. In 1993, one of the floats featured an Elvis Presley impersonator. In all, there will surely be more than fifty floats and fifty bands—and well over ten thousand marchers.

A classic inaugural parade picture. Here is the U.S. Army's Old Fife and Drum Corps, in 1989, with the U.S. Capitol in the background. **The Old Fife and Drum Corps, U.S. Army.**

Grover Cleveland watched the 1885 parade from a huge reviewing stand, directly in front of the White House, which can be seen in the background. **Library of Congress,** Prints and Photographs Division, John F. Jarvis, publisher, reproduction number LC-USZ62-12572.

Spectators will line the parade route. Most will be supporters of the new president, but protesters might make their presence known, too. In short, many different aspects of American life will be a part of the parade. For the new president and first family, as well as for all the participants in the parade, it will be an afternoon to remember.

From Spontaneity to Precision

The first time that an inaugural parade was a part of the official proceedings of the day was at James Madison's celebration in 1809. In a simple but stately presentation, on the way from his home to the Capitol, Madison received an escort from nine cavalry and militia companies. This accompaniment seemed a natural outgrowth from the spontaneous escorts given to George Washington in 1789 and Thomas Jefferson in 1805.

Some soldiers Washington had commanded during the Revolutionary War escorted him through a few New York streets on the first Inauguration Day. They cheered as they marched seven blocks to the only other official inaugural event of the day, a religious service at St. Paul's Chapel. After Jefferson's second inauguration, the president got aboard his favorite horse and was accompanied along Pennsylvania Avenue by mechanics from the local navy yard, members of Congress, diplomats, and other citizens from all walks of life. A military band played music along the way. This was the first time a president had led a parade down Washington's most famous street.

The parades grew as the years passed. By the time of William Henry Harrison's inauguration in 1841, political clubs and marching societies would regularly come to Washington for the parade. That was also the first year that floats were a part of the festivities. At James Buchanan's inaugural parade in 1857, one of the floats was an amazing replica of the ship *Constitution*. Cadets from the U.S. Military Academy and midshipmen from the U.S. Naval Academy marched in the inaugural parade for the first time at Ulysses S. Grant's second inauguration in 1873. That year marked the first time that the official parade took place after the ceremony. Up until then, the procession to the Capitol and the parade had really been just one event.

In future years, the parades continued to get larger. Marching bands were added, and the parades started to include herds of livestock, fife and drum corps, and minority groups. It wasn't long before the crowd of people that came to Washington for the big ceremony every four years knew fully that the parade had become one of the major events of the day.

Presidentially Sealed with a Kiss

During the years of the Civil War and World War I, the military groups who marched in the parade were present for more than mere show; there was the potential protection of Presidents Lincoln and Wilson to consider. But Lincoln's first inaugural parade, in 1861, produced one moment that everyone who saw it—and particularly those who participated in it—would long remember.

After his inaugural address, Abraham Lincoln went to the White House for a reception. There, he met thirty-four young girls who had been on a large red, white, and blue, draped float during the parade earlier that day. Each one of those girls represented one of the thirty-four states in our country at that time, and each girl was wearing a laurel wreath on her head. At the White House, the girls excitedly surrounded the new president. Lincoln then picked up each girl and gave each one a kiss!

It was at Lincoln's second inauguration, in 1865, that Native Americans and African Americans marched in the parade for the first time. Indian dancers would remain on the parade scene for many years to come. And, speaking of Indians, spectators at Benjamin Harrison's 1889 inaugural parade thoroughly enjoyed a show performed by Buffalo Bill and his "wild west" troop.

The Big Parade

Without question, Theodore Roosevelt was one of the most popular presidents in our history. He had already lived a colorful life even before he became our nation's youngest president at the age of forty-two, following the assassination of William McKinley in 1901. He was an early environmentalist and loved to hike. He had been head of the New York City Police Board, governor of New York, and assistant secretary of the navy. And, he had served as a lieutenant colonel in the Spanish-American War in 1898, leading a group of soldiers known as the Rough Riders.

Roosevelt became the first president who had succeeded to the high office upon the death of his predecessor to then be elected in his own right. It seemed like everyone wanted to be a part of his inaugural parade on March 4, 1905. The program that day described the parade as the event Washington visitors "come to see, and what they all want to see ... this conglomerate and glorious pageant of soldiery and civilians which will march down the Avenue to the music of a hundred bands and to the honor of a newly inaugurated American President."

And what a parade it was! After the usual military groups marched, the fun began. There were Roosevelt's old buddies, the Rough Riders, and other veterans from that war, wearing their old uniforms. More than twenty-five political clubs were present. Coal miners from Pennsylvania paraded, dressed in their normal miners' working clothes, caps, and lamps. There were rail splitters from Ohio, the Union League of Maryland, and an organization called the Modern Woodmen of America.

There was also a group of cowboys from South Dakota, a flambeau club from Minnesota, and some lancers from New Jersey, along with youth groups and high school and college students wearing caps and gowns. The 1905 program lists three of the final parade participants as the "Elizabeth City County (colored) Republican Club" from Hampton, Virginia, the "Butler Zonaves (colored)" from Washington, D.C., and the "Coronella Republican Club (colored)" from Baltimore. The Coronellas' uniforms consisted of overcoats, derby hats, black trousers, gloves, and canes.

The music was continuous, and everyone had a great time. It was undoubtedly the most spectacular parade up to that time, one that would set the tone for inaugural parades of the future.

Desperate White House Wives

Through 1905, a woman's place in the procession to and from the Capitol on Inauguration Day—even a first lady's place—had been in the background. History dictated that, after the inaugural ceremonies had been completed, the new president would leave the Capitol and ride down Pennsylvania Avenue with the outgoing president.

But in 1909, First Lady Helen Herron "Nellie" Taft broke new ground when she took the ride with the new president, William Howard Taft. Most of the old-time traditionalists were outraged by this behavior, but Mrs. Taft said that she enjoyed doing what no woman had previously done.

Eight years later, in 1917, President and Mrs. Wilson became the first couple to ride together in both directions, from the White House to the Capitol for the ceremonies and back again. This would become a tradition in inauguration years when the president had been re-elected and there was thus no change in power.

The 1917 parade included, among its marchers, many of the "new Americans"—immigrants who had come to America at the beginning of the twentieth century. In the parade program, they were described as the "Polish American Societies, Syrian American Clubs, Allied Jewish Societies and the Sons of Italy." Also, in 1917, women marched in the inaugural parade for the very first time, suffragists who had already gained the right to vote in a few states in our country. The suffragists'

When William and Nellie Taft traveled together from the Capitol back to the White House following the 1909 ceremony, it was first time that a president had taken this ride with the first lady, rather than with the outgoing president. **Library of Congress,** Prints and Photographs Division, Keystone View Company, reproduction number LC-USZ62-7634.

presence in the parade vividly demonstrated how our country had started to change its attitude about the issue of women's rights.

Just four years earlier, in 1913, the same suffragists were only allowed to march in Washington on the day *prior* to Wilson's first inauguration. On that date—March 3, 1913—an estimated five to eight thousand suffragists had marched on Pennsylvania Avenue from the U.S. Capitol to the White House for the purpose of gaining attention to their cause. Many spectators were sympathetic to the women; but a large number of onlookers were upset, either because they opposed the idea of women voting or because they objected to the timing of the march. Consequently, many of the suffragists were insulted, slapped, spit upon, or even beaten. Although the parade organizers had obtained a police permit for their march, the police did not protect them from being attacked.

Those 1913 events led to the police chief being fired and to new support for the rights of women. In 1917, those same suffragists were marching in the regular inaugural parade. By the next national election, in 1920, all women in our country would have the right to vote.

Nixon's the One

Richard Nixon, the only president to ever resign in disgrace, also holds the distinction of being the first president to have his inaugural parades disrupted by demonstrators. During his campaign for the presidency, Nixon had said that he had "a secret plan to end the war in Vietnam." But demonstrators on his Inauguration Day were not of the belief that Nixon's plan meant ending the war by returning our troops home.

Hundreds of anti-Vietnam War protestors came to Washington on January 20, 1969. Small American flags were burned along Pennsylvania Avenue. Some of the loud chants that could be heard were "Four more years of death," "Sieg heil, inaugurate the pig," and "Nixon's the one—the number one war criminal," mimicking Nixon's 1968 campaign slogan "Nixon's the One." A handful of sticks, stones, cans, bottles, and smoke bombs were even hurled toward Nixon's limousine as it headed down Pennsylvania Avenue, but no objects hit the presidential car.

Protesters were on one side of the street, with the District of Columbia Police and 82nd Airborne Division paratroopers on the other side. There were three thousand members of the local police, along with five thousand regular troops and one thousand national guardsmen deployed in the Capitol that day. The tight security included the taping shut of all mailboxes near the parade route. A total of eighty-one people were arrested.

During the next four years, the war escalated under Nixon. On January 20, 1973, the date of his second inauguration, the protests were bigger and actually took place all over the world. Demonstrators that day chanted, "Nixon fascist assassin" in front of the U.S. Embassy in Paris, bringing traffic to a halt along the Champs-Élysées. There were protests against Nixon in Mexico City, Hong Kong, Tokyo, Stockholm, Helsinki, Berlin, New Delhi, and all across the United States.

In Washington itself, police estimated that there were twenty-five thousand to thirty thousand demonstrators. There were groups such as the Vietnam Veterans Against the War, Women's Strike for Peace, Students for a Democratic Society, and lots of citizens who were simply tired of war. Large rallies were held at the Lincoln and Washington Memorials. A group called the Youth International Party, or Yippies, marched behind a twenty-five-foot-long papier-mâché rat while singing the Mickey Mouse Club song. The Yippies indicated that the rat symbolized Richard Nixon.

Antiwar handbills were distributed to spectators along the parade route. When the presidential limousine drove by, it was showered with eggs and debris. Washington police made thirty-six arrests during the affair.

The last known time that people had tried to countermarch at an inauguration was at Franklin Pierce's parade in 1853. A small group of unemployed people had been quickly dispersed that day. Then, in 1997, at Bill Clinton's parade, three women and two men "streaked" with bare chests onto the parade route, saying that they were animal rights activists. All were quickly arrested and charged with crossing a police line.

Walking the Walk

The most memorable moment of President Jimmy Carter's 1977 Inauguration occurred after the Capitol ceremonies and at the beginning of the parade. At 1:24 p.m., just three minutes after entering the presidential limousine, and without advance warning, the new president and the first lady, Rosalynn Carter, exited their car and began to walk down Pennsylvania Avenue. Everyone in the crowd of people lining the street excitedly spread the word: "They're walking! Jimmy and Rosalynn are walking!" In fact, the couple walked the entire parade route, a mile and a half, and their walk lasted forty-three minutes. Finally, at 2:07 p.m., the Carters' walk ended when they entered the inaugural parade reviewing stand in front of the White House.

The idea for the walk had originated with Senator William Proxmire of Wisconsin, who had suggested that it would be a fine example of the nation's need for improved physical fitness. But President Carter felt that the walk had an even more profound meaning. "I began to realize that the symbolism of our leaving the armored car would be much more far-reaching than simply to promote exercise," Carter later reminisced. "I remembered the angry demonstrators who had habitually confronted recent Presidents and Vice Presidents, furious over the Vietnam War and later the revelations of Watergate.

"I wanted to provide a vivid demonstration of my confidence in the people as far as security was concerned, and I felt a simple walk would

In 1977, Jimmy and Rosalynn Carter became the only president and first lady to walk the entire inaugural parade route. The crowd cheered them for the entire mile and a half. **Jimmy Carter Library.**

be a tangible indication of some reduction in the imperial status of the President and his family."

The Carters are the only first family to walk the entire distance. But Barbara and George Bush, in 1989, and Hillary and Bill Clinton, in 1993 and 1997, walked part of the way—and Laura and George W. Bush walked the last few hundred feet, in front of their supporters, before reaching the reviewing stand in both 2001 and 2005.

Hail to the Thief

When President George W. Bush's limousine reached Freedom Plaza along Pennsylvania Avenue during his 2001 inaugural parade, he witnessed something none of his predecessors had ever seen: a large area along the parade route where protesters actually outnumbered his supporters. Unlike the scattered and rather disorganized protests during the Nixon inaugurations of 1969 and 1973, the protesters had been granted permits to demonstrate along Pennsylvania Avenue.

The 2000 presidential election had been one for the history books. Democratic Party candidate Al Gore received more than a half million more votes than Republican George W. Bush. But the Electoral College vote was close, and the election would be decided by the twenty-five electoral votes from the state of Florida. There were many disputed votes from that state, and Florida officials began to recount the ballots. A full five weeks after the election had ended, the United States Supreme Court ruled in a 5-4 decision to end further counting of the votes, thereby giving Bush the election win. It was the first time since Benjamin Harrison's 1888 victory that a candidate with fewer popular votes had, nevertheless, been elected president. The delay and disputed result also evoked memories of Thomas Jefferson, in 1800; John Quincy Adams, in 1824; and Rutherford B. Hayes, in 1876.

An estimated twenty thousand people arrived in Washington on Bush's Inauguration Day to demonstrate their displeasure. They were met by the largest security force in inauguration history up to that time: ten thousand uniformed and plainclothes officers from the District of Columbia, surrounding states, and federal agencies.

A sea of protest banners greeted Bush as he reached Freedom Plaza. Signs read, "Hail to the Thief," "Commander in Thief," "Selected, Not Elected," "Gore by 500,000—Bush by 1," "Supreme Injustice," and "Say thank you to the nice Supreme Court, Georgie."

One demonstrator threw an egg that hit Bush's car, and four green apples and a plastic water bottle were tossed in the direction of the presidential limousine. Another person threw a rotten tomato at the D.C. police chief. But, for the most part, the protests were peaceful. Although the National Guard had been mobilized, and police were prepared for as many as five thousand detentions and arrests, the Guard was never actually called in; only five people were arrested all day.

More protests awaited President Bush at his second inaugural parade in 2005. There was unprecedented security that day, as it was the first such ceremony following the September 11, 2001 terrorist attack on United States soil and the subsequent war in Iraq.

Washington was an armed camp, with more than six thousand police officers and seven thousand U.S. troops patrolling the streets. Roadblocks were erected all over the city, and inauguration spectators were detained and questioned before being allowed to enter the ceremony area or the parade route along Pennsylvania Avenue. The lines were long, and many spectators never made it to their seats. Along the parade route, protesters held signs reading "W is for War," "Worst President Ever," "With charity to none, with malice toward all," and "Inaugural Charade." Many of the demonstrators were upset with the estimated $40 million being spent by Bush supporters to stage lavish inaugural festivities during a time of war. An organization called "Turn Your Back on Bush" did just that–facing the other way when the presidential limousine drove by. The police pepper-sprayed hundreds of protesters and bystanders, and they arrested seventy-nine people.

Don't Rain on My Parade

Since 1809, the inaugural parade has been a planned part of Inauguration Day, with only a couple of exceptions. In 1921, President-elect Warren G. Harding decided not to have a parade because he was concerned about the health of President Woodrow Wilson, who was still suffering from a recent stroke. Then, in 1945, when our nation was still involved in World War II, no parade was planned or held.

Given the reality that our presidential inaugurations have always been scheduled during winter months, it shouldn't be surprising to know that plenty of parades have taken place in poor weather conditions—mud, rain, sleet, and snow. At Ulysses S. Grant's second inaugural parade, in 1873, for example, the cold weather caused valves in the musical instruments to ice up. The pinnacle of wintry inaugurations was probably William Howard Taft's ceremony in 1909. It had snowed heavily in the morning, enough to force the ceremony indoors to the Senate chamber. The snow lessened a bit in the afternoon, Pennsylvania Avenue was shoveled clear, and the parade went on as planned.

But on two occasions, in 1833 and 1985, terrible weather forced the cancellations of the parades following the second inaugurations of Andrew Jackson and Ronald Reagan. A windchill factor well below zero and a fear of participants and spectators getting frostbite were the problems in 1985. So instead, an indoor celebration was hastily organized at a Washington sports arena. Thirty-three bands had hoped to be part of that year's outdoor parade. When the event was moved inside, just five of those bands got the opportunity to play their music.

IV

The Inaugural Ball

It's Party Time!

D ay has given way to night and everyone is ready to dress up and have a big party. Sure, there will be fireworks at night, bright enough to light up the entire Washington mall. But it's the inaugural ball that the visitors to Washington desire to attend. There, they can dress up, see and be seen, just as in the early days of our history.

There have been times, mostly in the first half of the twentieth century, when there was no inaugural ball. There have been other years when there was a big open house at the White House, bigger than any ball might have been. But now, the inaugural ball is a regular part of the inauguration celebration. In fact, the number of inaugural balls has ballooned to double-digit figures at some recent inaugurations. Bill Clinton's 1997 festivities included a record fourteen such parties, held at hotels, museums, and Union Station.

The number of inaugural balls dropped to nine in 2001, but one of them was considered the "in" place to be: George W. Bush's "Texas Black Tie and Boots Inaugural Ball." Celebrities appearing included singers Lyle Lovett, George Strait, Tanya Tucker, and the Beach Boys; former Dallas Cowboys' quarterbacks Roger Staubach and Troy Aikman; golfer Ben Crenshaw and soccer star Mia Hamm. During the ball, Lee Greenwood sang his hit, "God Bless the USA," and the new president told the crowd, "I love you! And I love Texas! And I love my wife!" In 2005, with the country at war in Iraq, a new ball was added. It was called the Commander-in-Chief Ball, designed to give Bush a chance to mingle with some of our troops and their families.

Seventy-five thousand guests paid $150 each for their tickets in 1997, a far cry from the $4 cost for a ticket to the 1809 inaugural ball celebrating James Madison, or even the $5 charge for Franklin D. Roosevelt's 1933 party, held during the middle of the Great Depression. In the early days, the food at the ball would be superb, often including delicacies from Europe. What can inaugural ball guests expect in the way of food nowadays? Not much—and perhaps nothing at all! In 1997, there were free cookies and brownies at some of the parties. There was a cash bar at many of the balls. Indeed, most of the guests were surprised to find that their admission charge included no hors d'oeuvres. Potato chips could be purchased for $1.50, a small plastic glass of wine for $4, and water for $2. In 2005, the liquid refreshment included warm champagne and $5 beers.

Then, there are the entrees: For $5.50, guests can purchase little plastic boxes with choices such as pasta primavera, ham and cheese sandwiches on dry biscuits, or turkey and pesto on a croissant. In 2001, the party planners for George W. Bush indicated that the food was being served on "upscale plastic ware."

The guests will find that the room is overcrowded, with very little space to dance. There won't be nearly enough chairs to sit on. A guest who checks his or her coat may soon second-guess that decision, as the room can get cold and trying to reclaim the coat later can be a tedious undertaking. Of course, there is a lot of inaugural ball folklore regarding people losing their coats and hats. Abraham Lincoln lost his hat at Zachary Taylor's ball in 1849. In 1869, at Ulysses S. Grant's first inaugural ball, illiterate workers mixed up everyone's coat claims, leading to fights among the men and tears among the women.

Dwight and Mamie Eisenhower and their guests pose for a picture at an inaugural ball in 1953. **Dwight D. Eisenhower Library,** National Park Service photograph.

All of this can come as a bit of shock to one who assumes that an inaugural ball has something to do with Cinderella or royalty. Nancy Reagan wrote about the 1981 celebrations, "When they hear the words 'inaugural ball,' most people think of a grand ballroom with a huge dance floor and a lot of people dancing and enjoying themselves. I know I did. But the reality is very different: Crowds of people are jammed together, shoulder to shoulder, just standing there; there's no way you can dance, and it's so noisy that you can't even hear the orchestra."

President Lyndon B. Johnson expressed the same sentiments in 1965 when he said, "Never have so many paid so much to dance so little." Then, with a passing reference to the theme of his administration, Johnson added, "One thing I can say about the Great Society—it sure is crowded!"

So, then, what can guests expect to enjoy for their money? There might be some good entertainment. Some of the performers in 1997 were Sheryl Crow, Kenny G, Aretha Franklin, the Isley Brothers, Chuck Berry, Hootie and the Blowfish, Bo Diddley, and the Drifters. The swing bands of Tommy Dorsey and Guy Lombardo performed in 2001. But the real highlight of each inaugural ball is when the president arrives.

The president and spouse will undoubtedly make an appearance at every one of the balls. They will waltz around the stage and thank everyone for coming. If the president has some musical talent, such as Bill Clinton playing the saxophone or Richard Nixon playing the piano, the guests might get to hear a few notes. But don't expect the president to stay very long; there are many other balls to visit and guests to thank.

In 2001, writers for the Associated Press put a stopwatch to the amount of time that George and Laura Bush danced with each other at each of the nine balls. Dancing mostly to the notes of a song called "Waltz Across Texas," the couple danced for 29 seconds at the first ball, 46 seconds at the second ball, followed by 56, 67, 50, 48, 38, 50 and 49 seconds at each succeeding ball. When asked why he was cutting the dances so short, Bush said, "I want you to know it's hard to dance on carpet. That's my first excuse. My second excuse is that I'm a lousy dancer."

At his second inauguration in 2005, President and Mrs. Bush went to ten balls and danced a total of eight minutes and fifty-four seconds. Before their first dance that evening, Bush indicated "it may be the first time in four years" that he had danced with the first lady. The couple arrived back at the White House at 10:03 p.m., an hour and a half ahead of schedule.

A Tough Ticket

In the years from 1789 through 1809, the inaugural ball evolved from an afterthought to a full-fledged official event of the day. There was a ball held following George Washington's inauguration, but it didn't take place until a week after the swearing-in ceremonies and, consequently, many historians do not consider it to be an official part of inauguration history. Similarly, another ball, held after Washington's 1793 ceremony, is considered to be unofficial because it was only for members of Congress. Nevertheless, those early parties set the tone for the official inaugural balls that began in earnest on James Madison's big day in 1809.

The 1789 party, held on lower Broadway near Wall Street at New York's Dancing Assemblies, was said to have been "attended by some three hundred persons of distinction." The men wore colonial dress and wigs, and the women wore elaborate gowns. Before and after each dance, the guests bowed and curtsied to the new president. The ladies present at the affair carried with them a fan with a profile of George Washington on it—a gift from the French government to all present at the affair. As for Washington himself, he danced two cotillions and a minuet. Observers commented upon "his ease and grace of manner."

The first official ball in Washington, in 1809, helped establish First Lady Dolley Madison's reputation as a great party hostess. It was held at Long's Hotel, the present location of the Library of Congress. By all accounts, it was the social event of the era, attended by handpicked, high society guests from Washington, Georgetown, Baltimore, and Philadelphia. President and Mrs. Madison arrived at the ball in a coach drawn by four horses. The menu included champagne, brandy punch, terrapin, wild game, oysters, Virginia hams, cheeses, "Meringue Parisian" and "Charlotte Chantilly." The dancing went on until midnight, to the delight of just about everyone except one future president, John Quincy Adams. In Adams's opinion, "the crowd was excessive, the heat oppressive, and the entertainment bad."

On the whole, though, the first official inaugural ball was considered an overwhelming success. But the guest of honor, President Madison, was somewhat less enthusiastic about the evening. A full eighteen years older than his wife, and with evidently less energy, James Madison commented that night, "I would rather be home in bed."

The Wildest Party

A ndrew Jackson and Franklin D. Roosevelt are the only two presidents who did not attend their own inaugural balls. Roosevelt suffered from polio and was represented at the 1933 celebration by his wife, Eleanor. There were no balls following Roosevelt's other three inaugurations, due to the Great Depression and World War II. Jackson, too, suffered from poor health through much of his later life and didn't attend his inaugural balls in either 1829 or 1833. In fact, following his second inauguration, Jackson simply went to bed without even eating dinner.

But Jackson did host an open house at the White House following his first inauguration in 1829, one that is possibly the most famous inauguration party in history. This was the day that Jackson, the "People's President," had gained the presidency, the day when the crowd of people in both finery and rags had come to Washington to wish "Old Hickory" well. All of these well-wishers were invited by Jackson to come and meet him personally at the White House.

And in they went! People "from the highest and most polished down to the most vulgar and gross in the nation" arrived at the new president's residence, much to the chagrin of Washington traditionalists, who felt that the uneducated and illiterate were about to take over the government. The visitors trampled into the White House with their muddy boots and made a major mess of the fine rugs and satin chairs. Waiters carrying punch collided with guests who were surging forward to get inside, causing the punch to spill all over the furniture. Chairs were

"President's Levee, or all Creation going to the White House, Washington" is artist Robert Cruikshank's depiction of the mass of people that created a near riot at Andrew Jackson's reception in 1829. **Library of Congress,** Rare Book and Special Collections Division, reproduction number LC-USZC4-970.

permanently wrecked from the sheer weight of the people standing on them, trying to get a glimpse of Jackson.

The mob scene got only bigger. China was smashed, crystal was broken, fights broke out, and women fainted. Some people were battling for food, others to touch the new president. When Jackson's personal safety came into question, several people encircled the president and escorted him out of the White House through an open window. The large gathering of citizens at the White House was finally persuaded to leave the residence when someone got the brilliant idea of placing the big tubs of whiskey onto the White House south lawn. Slowly but surely, the visitors left and the rowdy party came to a merciful conclusion.

Yes, in 1829, the mostly well-meaning crowd had gotten overly exuberant. But the people had also demonstrated for all time that the spirit of America at a presidential inauguration would mean more than just a celebration for the powerful and rich. People from all walks of life would want to be a part of inaugurations in the future, including the balls that had previously been only for the rich and powerful. When Zachary Taylor was inaugurated in 1849, his political party, the Whigs, decided to have an exclusive ball. The Democrats and the citizens of Washington were so opposed to this return to past traditions that an opposition ball was organized, called "The National Inauguration Ball Without Distinction of Party."

The Loneliest Night

There was little joy in the White House during Franklin Pierce's term as president, from 1853 to 1857. His wife, Jane, was preoccupied with mourning the death of their three children throughout the entire period, and she lived in virtual seclusion. Because their third child had died in a train crash just two months before the ceremony, Mrs. Pierce did not even come to her husband's inauguration. There was no inaugural ball on Pierce's inauguration night.

Although his predecessor, Millard Fillmore, did everything possible to try to make Pierce feel comfortable, the new president spent his first night in office—March 4, 1853—in a nearly desolate White House. The carpets had been left muddy. Pierce couldn't find any dishes, and, for some reason, the lighting wasn't working. Even the servants went to bed before anyone told the new president where he should sleep! Fumbling around the place with his secretary, Sidney Webster, Pierce lit a candle, found a room, and then said, "You'd better turn in here, Sidney. I'll try to find a bed somewhere across the hall."

The Runs for the White House

James Buchanan's inaugural ball was a truly spectacular affair. The dancing went on until dawn beneath a structure specially built for the occasion, located in Washington's Judiciary Square. The walls were lined with red, white, and blue draperies and with flags from all over the world. The guests "consumed 3,000 quarts of champagne, 400 gallons of oysters, 500 quarts of chicken salad, 1,200 quarts of ice cream, 500 quarts of jelly, 60 saddles of mutton, 16 sides of beef, 75 hams, 125 beef tongues, and pyramids of pâtés and hors d'oeuvres." The building had beautiful chandeliers and, instead of candles, gas was used for illumination for the first time at an inaugural ball.

But there was another kind of gas permeating the environment that night. President Buchanan was suffering from a gastrointestinal ailment that was being passed around Washington. The press called it the "National Hotel disease" because it was thought to have been caused by rats that were contaminating that hotel's water supply. Buchanan had attended a number of functions there and, during the days leading up to the inauguration, he had been suffering from a bad case of diarrhea. Naval surgeon Jonathan Foltz was near Buchanan the entire day and evening, prepared to render treatment when and if it became necessary.

Buchanan's inauguration was also the first ever to be photographed. But fortunately, the only known photos of the new president from that day are of the ceremony at the Capitol.

A Historic Greeting and Compliment

On the evening of March 4, 1865, the night of his second inauguration, President Abraham Lincoln held a public reception at the White House. It was estimated that he shook hands with six thousand people in just three hours.

One of the visitors who came to the White House that night to greet Lincoln was Frederick Douglass, the great African American leader in the battle against slavery. At first, the police were concerned and didn't want to let Douglass inside, but Lincoln insisted. As Douglass entered, Lincoln told those around him, "Here comes my friend Douglass." The president then turned to him.

"I am glad to see you," Lincoln said. "I saw you in the crowd today, listening to my address. There is no man in the country whose opinion I value more than yours." Lincoln desired to know what Douglass had thought of the "with malice toward none, with charity for all" speech.

Douglass then said, "Mr. Lincoln, it was a sacred effort."

"I'm glad you liked it," responded the president.

This had been the first time in history that a president of the United States had greeted and sought the opinion of a free black man inside the White House.

Who Is Buried at
Grant's Inaugural Balls?

The 1873 inaugural ball, celebrating President Ulysses S. Grant's second inauguration, was held in a temporary wooden structure in Judiciary Square, behind the Treasury Building. It took place on the second-coldest Inauguration Day in history, the high temperature reaching only sixteen degrees. There were strong winds, sleet, and snow. That record was broken in 1985 when the temperature was just seven degrees.

The problem in 1873 was that no one had made any arrangements to have the structure heated. Musicians had difficulty when violin strings snapped because they were too cold. Couples were forced to attempt to dance with their coats and hats still on. The food consisted of frozen turkeys, frozen oysters, and frozen drinks. People left early because it was simply too cold inside the makeshift ballroom.

Then there were the poor canaries. A flock of one hundred of the pretty birds had been brought to Washington from the South with plans that they would chirp away, making lovely sounds for Grant and his guests. Unfortunately, hardly anyone noticed when the canaries froze to death in their cages.

This was not the only time there were problems at an inaugural ball for President Grant. Four years earlier, mismanagement and lack of security had led to hundreds of guests at the ball losing their hats, coats and other valuables. The building was too small to accommodate all the ticket holders. People fell during a stampede for food, chaos that spilled over even into the kitchen area itself. There was no room for anyone to dance, and a mob scene ensued when the stairways became jammed, resulting in many of the ladies having their gowns ripped or even completely torn off!

Big Men, Big Parties

Some of the most elegant inaugural balls in our history took place between 1885 and 1909 at Washington's Pension Office, a structure now known as the National Building Museum. According to the 1901 program for William McKinley's second inauguration, "The magnificent court of this immense building affords suitable accommodations for the thousands who gather to make notable this great social feature of the induction of a Chief Executive into an office, which is the highest a republic can give. The Inaugural ball is a time-honored and always enjoyable function. The newly announced President attends with the members of his personal and official family, and leads the opening grand march. It forms a fitting and spectacular climax to a day of so much importance to the whole people."

It seems that the decorations for the inaugural ballrooms in those days were made with immaculate detail. Here's how the 1901 Inauguration program described that year's room decorations: "The general color effect will be a most delicate shade of yellow, known as old ivory. The ceiling will be a canopy of gracefully looped bunting, studded with innumerable incandescent lights burning within frosted glass. There will be no glare of dazzling arc lights, but an artistic mellow glow from the incandescent bulbs. The balconies which surround the court, the grand columns that reach from tiled floor to arching roof, will all be decorated lavishly by the most skilled artisans."

William and Ida McKinley led the opening march of that inaugural ball. All went well for a while, but the first lady then suffered a seizure and had to rest. She had been in rather poor health for a number of years. Her heart was weak, and she often suffered epileptic seizures. Nothing more drastic occurred that evening, however, and the couple still managed to enjoy the great event. In fact, Mrs. McKinley had some difficulty negotiating the stairs at their inaugural balls in both 1897 and 1901. Throughout their marriage, Ida's health was a major concern, and they always showed very open affection toward one another.

The setting was the same in 1909, the inaugural ball at the Pension Office for William Howard Taft. He was our nation's largest president at six feet, two inches and more than three hundred pounds. After enjoying a promenade concert of music by Von Weber, Greig, Chambers, Rossini, and Liszt—between 9 and 10 p.m.—here is what Taft had to eat at his party that immediately followed:

Chicken Consomme

Terrapin a la Baltimore

Cotolettes Perigourdine

Green Peas

Quails a l'Estouffade

Salad of Season

Fantaisie, Glace

Peaches Melba

Fancy Cakes

Bonbons Fourres

Cafe Noir

Ball Busters

Beginning in 1809, there were balls at every inauguration for the next one hundred years, with only three exceptions. There was none in 1821 because Elizabeth Monroe was not fond of social affairs. Franklin and Jane Pierce were still in mourning over the death of their third child at the time of the 1853 inauguration. Mrs. Pierce didn't even attend the ceremony, and the new president wasn't in much of a party mood either. And in 1877, there was so much dispute about the results of the election between Rutherford B. Hayes and Samuel J. Tilden that a ball was probably the last thing on anyone's mind.

But after a series of successful balls through William Howard Taft's celebration in 1909, everything changed in 1913. President Woodrow Wilson and his wife believed that a ball would jeopardize the solemnity of the occasion of an inauguration. Wilson was a man who had never owned a vehicle other than a bicycle. He preferred the simple life and did not wish to make himself and his family the center of attention. In 1921, President Warren G. Harding chose not to have any celebration, instead stating, "It will be most pleasing to me to be simply sworn in, speak briefly my plight of faith to the country and turn at once to the work which will be calling." An era of no official inaugural balls thus began. There were some private parties and so-called "Charity Balls" during the 1920s, and one inaugural ball was held in 1933. But the Great Depression and World War II seemed to dampen any real passion for again holding inaugural balls on a regular basis.

Finally, in 1949, President Harry Truman brought back the tradition, and there have been inaugural balls ever since. The number of parties has grown at virtually every inauguration, rising to four for the first time at Dwight D. Eisenhower's second celebration, in 1957, and all the way up to a record number of fourteen on the night of President Bill Clinton's second inauguration, in 1997.

V

Sudden Death
(and Resignation)

No Party of Five

The inaugurations that have taken place on a planned day (April 30 for Washington's 1789 ceremony, March 4 for every inauguration between 1793 and 1933, and January 20 from 1937 until the present) have comprised the vast majority of the inaugurations in our nation's history. Every four years, on a set day and at the designated time of twelve o'clock noon, we know there will be a presidential inauguration—a big celebration from morning until night.

But, sadly, not all of our presidents have come into office with such ceremonies. Not all of them have been able to enjoy the cheers of the crowd as they took the oath and gave their inaugural addresses, passed by on parade, and waltzed at a ball.

On nine occasions, our country has had a sudden inauguration, one which was unplanned and unanticipated. These were the times when we called upon our vice president to assume the office of president because his predecessor had passed away or, in the case of Gerald R. Ford, because his predecessor resigned due to a political scandal. Each of these nine men took the oath of office, then served out the remaining years of his predecessor's term. Four of them—Theodore Roosevelt, Calvin Coolidge, Harry S. Truman, and Lyndon B. Johnson—were subsequently elected to serve their own terms as president. Thus, Roosevelt in 1905, Coolidge in 1925, Truman in 1949, and Johnson in 1965 all were able to enjoy a traditional inauguration on the East Portico steps of the Capitol in Washington.

But there was never any party at all for five of our Presidents. John Tyler, Millard Fillmore, Andrew Johnson, Chester A. Arthur, and Gerald R. Ford finished out their terms and were never again elected to office. Of the five, only Ford was even nominated by his own party to run for president in the next election; he was defeated, in 1976, by Jimmy Carter.

A Humble Beginning

When William Henry Harrison died, just one month after his inauguration in 1841, John Tyler became the first vice president to rise to the presidency upon the death of his predecessor. Harrison had contracted pneumonia as the result of an overly long inaugural address and overzealous partying on his inauguration night.

Tyler was playing marbles with his children at their home near Williamsburg, Virginia, on April 4, 1841, when he learned of Harrison's death. According to legend, Tyler then said to them, "My children, by a deplored event, I am unexpectedly elevated to the presidency of the United States. You, as my children, of course, rise with me. I beg you ever to bear in mind that this promotion is only temporary. I must return to plain John Tyler—and may you never, as the president's children, either in thought, word or deed, do aught which you will regret to be told of afterwards, when you shall be nothing higher than plain John Tyler's children."

Some political leaders wanted to refer to Tyler as "acting president," but Tyler would have none of it. He declared that there was no Constitutional provision for an "acting president," and he insisted on taking the oath. Upon learning that Chief Justice Roger B. Taney was out of town, Tyler requested that another judge swear him in. Chief Justice of the United States District Court for the District of Columbia William Cranch administered the oath in Tyler's hotel suite in Washington on April 6, 1841.

The next president to die in office was Zachary Taylor, in 1850. Taylor had spent a long time in the hot sun at a July 4 celebration in 1850. He developed a stomach ailment and died five days later. This time, there was no question that Millard Fillmore would be the righteous successor as president. Fillmore took the oath of office in the House of Representatives on July 10, 1850. Ironically, the oath was once again administered by William Cranch, who thus became the only person other than a chief justice of the United States Supreme Court to swear in more than one president.

Assassination

Three times in the thirty-six years between 1865 and 1901, our nation's president was shot to death by an assassin. Each of these events was shocking and tragic. In each instance, the vice president was sworn into office within a very short time. On April 14, 1865, President Abraham Lincoln was shot while watching a play in Washington's Ford's Theatre by an actor who had sided with the Confederacy during the Civil War. When Lincoln died the next morning, Vice President Andrew Johnson was administered the oath of office by the chief justice in Johnson's residence at the Kirkwood House (hotel) in Washington.

President James A. Garfield was shot on July 2, 1881, by a disgruntled person seeking a political appointment. He was nursed for more than two months but passed away on September 19. Vice President Chester A. Arthur was at his residence in New York City when he was advised of the news. Arthur buried his face in his hands, put his head on a table, and cried. The next day, right there in his own home, he was sworn in by New York Supreme Court Judge John R. Brady. Two days later, at the vice president's room at the Capitol in Washington, Arthur was administered the oath a second time, by the chief justice.

On September 6, 1901, President William McKinley was shot by an anarchist while shaking hands with well-wishers at the Pan-American Exposition in Buffalo, New York. Vice President Theodore Roosevelt was on a hiking trip in the Adirondack Mountains in upper New York when he received word of McKinley's condition. Roosevelt canceled his trip and

Lyndon B. Johnson is sworn into office by U.S. District Judge Sarah T. Hughes, aboard Air Force One in Dallas, Texas, following the assassination of John F. Kennedy in 1963. Kennedy's widow, Jacqueline, is on Johnson's left. **Lyndon B. Johnson Library,** photo by Cecil Stoughton.

journeyed to Buffalo. When McKinley died, on September 14, Roosevelt was administered the presidential oath of office by United States Federal District Judge John R. Hazel. The brief ceremony took place in the home of Ansley Wilcox, a friend of Roosevelt. When Roosevelt concluded the oath, he added the words "and thus I swear."

By the year 1963, Americans who had grown up reading about the three previous assassinations in our history considered them to be just that—history. Certainly nothing like a presidential assassination could ever again occur in our more sophisticated society, or so some thought. But the nation was shocked beyond belief when our youngest elected president, John F. Kennedy, was shot to death during a presidential motorcade in Dallas, Texas, on November 22, 1963. Vice President Lyndon B. Johnson, who had been part of that same motorcade, was sworn in that afternoon aboard Air Force One. The oath was administered by United States Federal District Judge Sarah T. Hughes, the only woman to ever swear in a president.

The plane bearing Kennedy's coffin then flew from Dallas to Washington. Upon arriving in our nation's capital, President Johnson exited the plane and walked toward some microphones.

He made a statement to all Americans, both appropriate to the moment and similar to those other occasions when tragedy has led to a sudden inauguration. Johnson said, "This is a sad time for all people. We have suffered a loss that cannot be weighed. For me, it is a deep personal tragedy. I know the world shares the sorrow that Mrs. Kennedy and her family bear. I will do my best. That is all I can do. I ask for your help—and God's."

Father Knows Best

President Warren G. Harding died on August 2, 1923, in San Francisco. He had suffered food poisoning and developed pneumonia, complicated by a heart ailment. Vice President Calvin Coolidge learned of Harding's passing during the early morning hours of August 3, while he and his wife were spending the night at the home of his father, Col. John Coolidge, in Plymouth Notch, Vermont. Coolidge's father's house was very old. It had no electricity, no telephone, and no running water inside.

A telegram bearing the news of Harding's death had been sent to Bridgewater, eight miles from Plymouth Notch, and had been delivered to the Coolidge home by the local switchboard operator. Col. Coolidge went up the stairs, woke his son, and gave him the news. Shortly thereafter, the vice president received word from both the attorney general and the secretary of state that he should take the oath of office as soon as possible. Those telegrams from Washington included the wording of the oath, information that no one at the home knew by heart.

Coolidge's father was a notary public as well as the local justice of the peace. So, Col. John Coolidge administered the oath to his son at 2:47 a.m., by the light of an old kerosene lamp. It is the only time in our nation's history that a president was sworn into office by his father. Years later, when asked how he knew that he could administer the presidential oath to his son, Col. Coolidge responded, "I didn't know that I couldn't."

"Swearing-in of Calvin Coolidge by his Father" is artist Arthur I. Keller's rendering of the memorable kerosene lamplit ceremony in 1923. **Vermont Division for Historic Preservation, President Calvin Coolidge State Historic Site.**

President Coolidge wrote in his autobiography: "I do not know of any other case in history where the succession comes by election, where a father had administered to his son the qualifying oath of office. It seemed a simple and a natural thing to do at the time. Father was then, as always, a Notary Public. I can now realize something of the dramatic force of the event." Indeed, those early morning hours in Vermont truly captured the imagination of the American public as no prior inauguration had.

Although virtually all historians now recognize the validity of the oath taken at John Coolidge's home, the attorney general at the time, Harry M. Daugherty, began to have some reservations about its legitimacy. The solicitor general, James M. Beck, also had some doubts. They believed it possible that John Coolidge only had authority to swear in Vermont state officials. So, to be on the safe side, Calvin Coolidge was sworn in again on August 17, 1923, at the New Willard Hotel in Washington, where Coolidge was living (Mrs. Harding had not yet moved her belongings out of the White House). Justice Adolph A. Hoehling, of the Supreme Court of the District of Columbia, administered that second oath.

Are You Ready?

Franklin D. Roosevelt had been elected president four times and had been president for more than twelve years. Since he had taken our country through the Great Depression and World War II, it was difficult for many Americans to imagine anyone else as president. But on April 12, 1945, Roosevelt suddenly died of a cerebral hemorrhage. Harry S. Truman, a man who had been vice president for less than three months, was suddenly thrust into the presidency.

Roosevelt's wife, Eleanor, summoned Truman to the White House. Mrs. Roosevelt told him, "Harry, the president is dead." Truman then asked Mrs. Roosevelt, in a comforting way, "Is there anything I can do?"

Mrs. Roosevelt, having been first lady for more than twelve years and, knowing something about the difficult realities of being the nation's leader, then replied, "Is there anything *we* can do for *you*?—for you are the one in trouble now."

Chief Justice Harlan F. Stone swore in Truman as president that same day in the Cabinet Room of the White House. In asking Truman to repeat after him, Stone first said, "I, Harry Shipp Truman, do solemnly swear...." One of Truman's grandfathers had the middle name Shipp, but Truman's parents had given their son only a middle initial, S, rather than a full middle name. So, Truman responded to the chief justice by saying, "I, Harry S. Truman, do solemnly swear...." As Stone first recited the oath, Truman held his left hand under a Bible and his right hand

Harry S. Truman was inaugurated as president in the Cabinet Room of the White House, following Franklin D. Roosevelt's death in 1945. **Harry S. Truman Library,** photograph by Abbie Rowe, number 73-1909.

atop the book. But when Truman began to speak, he raised his right hand in the air, still holding the Bible with his left hand.

Truman told reporters the next day, "Boys, if you ever pray, pray for me now. I don't know if you fellows ever had a load of hay fall on you, but when they told me yesterday what had happened, I felt like the moon, the stars, and all the planets had fallen on me."

Nightmare on Pennsylvania Avenue

One of the least likely persons to ever become president was Gerald R. Ford. Ford had served in Congress for twelve terms and was certainly politically qualified. The thing that was different about Ford was that he became the only person to ever become president without having been elected either president or vice president. Ford had been appointed vice president by President Richard M. Nixon to replace Spiro T. Agnew, who had resigned the vice presidency while under criminal investigation.

Then, on August 8, 1974, President Nixon himself announced that he would resign because of the Watergate scandal, a series of misdeeds that included burglaries, cover-ups, and other abuses of power. By the time of the resignation, our nation had been consumed by Watergate news for more than two years.

"Our long national nightmare is over," Ford said the next day, when he was sworn in by the chief justice in the East Room of the White House. "Our Constitution works. Our great republic is a government of laws and not of men. Here, the people rule."

Ford also said, "I assume the presidency under extraordinary circumstances never experienced before by Americans. This is an hour of history that troubles our minds and hurts our hearts. Therefore, I feel it is my first duty to make an unprecedented compact with my countrymen. Not an inaugural address, not a fireside chat, not a campaign speech—

just a little straight talk among friends.... I am acutely aware that you have not elected me as your president by your ballots, and so I ask you to confirm me as your president with your prayers.... I have not sought this enormous responsibility, but I will not shirk it."

Some of Ford's first words as president, referring to the Watergate scandal as a "national nightmare," turned out to be the most famous he ever said. Yet, Ford nearly decided not to use that phrase. In a 1984 interview with Phil Jones of CBS News, which was not publicly released until after Ford's death in 2006, Ford revealed that his speechwriter Robert Hartmann had written the key words. "That phrase jarred me," Ford said in the interview. He then suggested to Hartmann, "We really ought not to use that. Let's not be too harsh. Let's not be too dramatic."

But Ford said Hartmann "really put his foot down." Hartmann told Ford, "That is an accurate expression of what has taken place, and you've got to keep it in your speech."

Ford thought about the matter further and discussed it with his wife Betty. Finally, Ford said, "We decided to leave it in. And boy, in retrospect, I'm awfully glad we did."

The End of the Affair

Some of the inaugural balls are ending, while others may go on until dawn. The new president, having made an appearance at each and every one of them, is finally winding down his Inauguration Day. It is time to go home.

It has become an American tradition for the outgoing president to leave a note in the White House for his successor. At the end of a long and exciting Inauguration Day, the new president arrives at the White House and opens a desk drawer. Inevitably, the note is waiting. Most of these words of wisdom have been along the lines of "Good luck in your new home" or "We hope you enjoy your stay here as much as we did."

In 1989, Ronald Reagan wrote a note to George Bush on stationery with the printed words "Don't let the turkeys get you down" at the top of the page. Reagan's words were: "Dear George, You'll have moments when you want to use this particular stationery. Well, go to it. George, I treasure the memories we share and wish you all the very best. You'll be in my prayers. God bless you and Barbara. I'll miss our Thursday lunches. Ron." Indeed, leaving the White House after four or eight years is often an emotional period for a president and his family. The good times are remembered fondly, but the reality that now is the time for someone new to occupy the position has sometimes been very painful, particularly for other members of the outgoing president's family. Nevertheless, almost every one has wished his successor well.

In 2001, George W. Bush arrived at the White House after the inaugural parade had ended. More than six hours had elapsed since he had taken the late morning ride to the Capitol with the outgoing president, Bill Clinton. During that time, pictures of the previous president and first lady had been removed. Armchairs, drapes, rugs, and sofas had been changed. Some of the walls had been painted, including those of the oval office, changed from a dominant color pattern of red and blue to new peach tones. Bush sat down and opened a desk drawer. There, he found the traditional congratulatory note from Clinton. Yet, there was something else that Bill Clinton wanted George W. Bush to have: attached to the note was a copy of the personal note left for Clinton eight years earlier by Bush's father.

When Benjamin Harrison replaced Grover Cleveland as president in 1889, a very different sort of message was sent to the White House staff. Cleveland's young wife, Frances, who had married Cleveland during his term in office, was packing up to make way for Harrison's move into the White House. Mrs. Cleveland told one of the members of the staff, "I want you to take good care of everything—the furnishings, the china, the crystal, the silver. I want to find everything just as it is now when my husband and I move back in here precisely four years from today."

Exactly four years later, on March 4, 1893, Mrs. Cleveland's prediction came true. Cleveland and Harrison rode from the White House to the Capitol together for the second inauguration in succession. The first time, Cleveland had sat on the right side as the outgoing president. In 1893, they switched sides. So far, Grover Cleveland is the only president in our history to serve two nonconsecutive terms.

Now, we again have a new president who has just been inaugurated. Democracy's big day has been one of transition and of celebration for a person and a nation. No one can yet possibly predict how long the new administration will last or how successful it will be. Our new president's first full day as our nation's leader is only a few hours away.

Inauguration Map

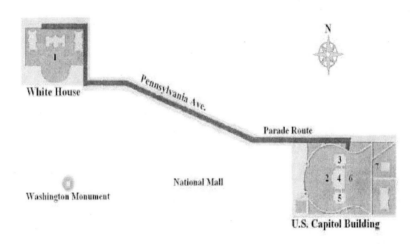

The above numbers refer to the sites where inaugurations have taken place:

(1) **White House:** 1877 Hayes (in the Red Room), 1945 Franklin D. Roosevelt (South Portico), 1945 Truman (Cabinet Room), 1957 Eisenhower (private Sunday ceremony in East Room), 1974 Ford (East Room), and 1985 Reagan (private Sunday ceremony in front of grand staircase).

(2) **U.S. Capitol West Front:** 1981–present.

(3) **U.S. Senate Chamber:** 1801 Jefferson, 1805 Jefferson, and 1909 Taft.

(4) **U.S. Capitol** (other than inside Senate or House chambers): 1881 Arthur (vice president's room), 1917 Wilson (Sunday ceremony in president's office), and 1985 Reagan (Rotunda).

(5) **U.S. House of Representatives Chamber:** 1809 Madison, 1813 Madison, 1821 Monroe, 1825 John Quincy Adams, 1833 Jackson, and 1850 Fillmore.

(6) **U.S. Capitol East Portico:** 1829–1877 (with exceptions listed here).

(7) **Platform outside Congress Hall** (where U.S. Supreme Court is now located): Monroe 1817.

Inauguration Chart

INAUGURAL NUMBER AND DATE	PRESIDENT	PARTY	AGE	SITE OF INAUG.	SWORN IN BY	WEATHER	# OF INAUG. BALLS	NOTABLE ASPECTS
1st April 30, 1789	George Washington	Federalist	57	New York City, Federal Hall (a)	New York State Chancellor Robert R. Livingston	59°, clear and cool	1 (b)	first inauguration
2nd March 4, 1793	George Washington	Federalist	61	Phil, PA, Congress Hall, U.S. Senate	U.S. Supreme Ct. Justice William Cushing		1 (c)	shortest inaugural address
3rd March 4, 1797	John Adams	Federalist	61	Phil, PA, House of Reps.	Chief Justice Oliver Ellsworth		0	first president to be sworn in by the chief justice
4th March 4, 1801	Thomas Jefferson	Democratic-Republican	57	Wash DC, U.S. Senate	Chief Justice John Marshall		0	first Washington inauguration; "We are all Federalists; we are all Republicans"

5th March 4, 1805	Thomas Jefferson	Democratic-Republican	61	Wash DC, U.S. Senate	Chief Justice John Marshall		0	first informal parade down Pennsylvania Avenue
6th March 4, 1809	James Madison	Democratic-Republican	57	Wash DC, House of Reps.	Chief Justice John Marshall		1	first official inaugural parade and first official inaugural ball
7th March 4, 1813	James Madison	Democratic-Republican	61	Wash DC, House of Reps.	Chief Justice John Marshall		1	during middle of War of 1812
8th March 4, 1817	James Monroe	Democratic-Republican	58	Wash DC, elevated platform outside Congress Hall	Chief Justice John Marshall	50°, warm and sunny	1	first fully outdoor inauguration
9th March 5, 1821	James Monroe	Democratic-Republican	62	Wash DC, House of Reps. (d)	Chief Justice John Marshall	28°, snow	0	first inauguration delayed to avoid Sunday ceremony; ceremony moved indoors because of poor weather

INAUGURAL NUMBER AND DATE	PRESIDENT	PARTY	AGE	SITE OF INAUG.	SWORN IN BY	WEATHER	# OF INAUG. BALLS	NOTABLE ASPECTS
10th March 4, 1825	John Quincy Adams	Democratic-Republican	57	Wash DC, House of Reps.	Chief Justice John Marshall		1	first son of a former president to become president; first president to wear long pants (rather than knickers) at his inauguration
11th March 4, 1829	Andrew Jackson	Democratic	61	Wash DC, East Portico	Chief Justice John Marshall	57°, warm and balmy	1	first inauguration at Capitol's East Portico; wildest inauguration party
12th March 4, 1833	Andrew Jackson	Democratic	65	Wash DC, House of Reps. (d)	Chief Justice John Marshall	29°, snow	1	ceremony moved indoors and inaugural parade canceled due to poor weather

	President	Party	Age	Location	Oath administered by	Weather		Notes
13th March 4, 1837	Martin Van Buren	Democratic	54	Wash DC, East Portico	Chief Justice Roger B. Taney	26°, sunny and brisk	2	first president born as an American citizen; first time the old and the new presidents rode together to Capitol ceremony
14th March 4, 1841	William Henry Harrison	Whig	68	Wash DC, East Portico	Chief Justice Roger B. Taney	48°, overcast and windy	3	longest inaugural address; caught pneumonia, died one month later
April 6, 1841	John Tyler	Whig	51	Wash DC, Brown's Indian Queen Hotel, Tyler's residence	William Cranch, chief judge, U.S. District Court for District of Columbia		—	first vice president to succeed to presidency upon death of predecessor
15th March 4, 1845	James K. Polk	Democratic	49	Wash DC, East Portico	Chief Justice Roger B. Taney	42°, rain	2	first inauguration to be reported by telegraph
16th March 5, 1849	Zachary Taylor	Whig	64	Wash DC, East Portico	Chief Justice Roger B. Taney	42°, cloudy with snow flurries	3	inauguration delayed one day to Monday

INAUGURAL NUMBER AND DATE	PRESIDENT	PARTY	AGE	SITE OF INAUG.	SWORN IN BY	WEATHER	# OF INAUG. BALLS	NOTABLE ASPECTS
July 10, 1850	Millard Fillmore	Whig	50	Wash DC, House of Reps.	William Cranch, chief judge, U.S. District Court for District of Columbia		—	oath administered by same substitute justice who had sworn in John Tyler
17th March 4, 1853	Franklin Pierce	Democratic	48	Wash DC, East Portico	Chief Justice Roger B. Taney	35°, snow and wind	0	only president to affirm the oath; memorized inaugural address
18th March 4, 1857	James Buchanan	Democratic	65	Wash DC, East Portico	Chief Justice Roger B. Taney	49°, sunny	1	first inauguration to be photographed
19th March 4, 1861	Abraham Lincoln	Republican	52	Wash DC, East Portico	Chief Justice Roger B. Taney	rain in morning, sunny in afternoon	1	massive military presence at inauguration

	President	Party	Age	Location	Chief Justice	Weather		Notes
20th March 4, 1865	Abraham Lincoln	Republican	56	Wash DC, East Portico	Chief Justice Salmon P. Chase	45°, rain before ceremony, then sun	1	"with malice toward none, with charity for all"; first inaugural parade to include African Americans
April 15, 1865	Andrew Johnson	Union	56	Wash DC, Kirkwood House (hotel), Johnson's residence	Chief Justice Salmon P. Chase		—	delivered his vice presidential speech while drunk just 42 days earlier
21st March 4, 1869	Ulysses S. Grant	Republican	46	Wash DC, East Portico	Chief Justice Salmon P. Chase	40°, rain before ceremony, then sun	1	much patriotic enthusiasm for first inauguration after Civil War
22nd March 4, 1873	Ulysses S. Grant	Republican	50	Wash DC, East Portico	Chief Justice Salmon P. Chase	16°, clear, windy and cold (morning low: 4°)	1	second coldest weather on Inauguration Day; first presidential reviewing stand at an inaugural parade; frozen food at inaugural ball

INAUGURAL NUMBER AND DATE	PRESIDENT	PARTY	AGE	SITE OF INAUG.	SWORN IN BY	WEATHER	# OF INAUG. BALLS	NOTABLE ASPECTS
March 3, 1877	Rutherford B. Hayes	Republican	54	Wash DC, Red Room at White House	Chief Justice Morrison R. Waite		—	only president to be sworn in a day early, privately at White House
23rd March 5, 1877	Rutherford B. Hayes	Republican	54	Wash DC, East Portico	Chief Justice Morrison R. Waite	35°, cloudy with light snow	0	public ceremony held two days later; first time an incoming president went to the White House to meet with outgoing president before procession to the Capitol
24th March 4, 1881	James A. Garfield	Republican	49	Wash, DC, East Portico	Chief Justice Morrison R. Waite	33°, snow before ceremony, then sunny and windy	1	first inauguration attended by the mother of a president; first inaugural parade reviewing stand in front of the White House

Date	President	Party	Age	Location	Oath Administered By	Weather		Notes
September 20, 1881	Chester A. Arthur	Republican	51	New York City, at Arthur's home	New York Supreme Court Judge John R. Brady		—	only president to be sworn in at his own home
September 22, 1881	Chester A. Arthur	Republican	51	Wash DC, VP's room at Capitol	Chief Justice Morrison R. Waite		—	sworn in again two days later at Capitol
25th March 4, 1885	Grover Cleveland	Democratic	47	Wash DC, East Portico	Chief Justice Morrison R. Waite	54°, sunny	1	like Pierce, memorized his inaugural address
26th March 4, 1889	Benjamin Harrison	Republican	55	Wash DC, East Portico	Chief Justice Melville W. Fuller	43°, rain	1	outgoing President Cleveland held umbrella over Harrison during rainy ceremony
27th March 4, 1893	Grover Cleveland	Democratic	55	Wash DC, East Portico	Chief Justice Melville W. Fuller	25°, snow and wind	1	only president to serve two non-consecutive terms
28th March 4, 1897	William McKinley	Republican	54	Wash DC, East Portico	Chief Justice Melville W. Fuller	40°, clear	1	first inauguration to be filmed and recorded with sound

INAUGURAL NUMBER AND DATE	PRESIDENT	PARTY	AGE	SITE OF INAUG.	SWORN IN BY	WEATHER	# OF INAUG. BALLS	NOTABLE ASPECTS
29th March 4, 1901	William McKinley	Republican	58	Wash DC, East Portico	Chief Justice Melville W. Fuller	47°, rain	1	recent war hero Theodore Roosevelt new vice president
September 14, 1901	Theodore Roosevelt	Republican	42	Buffalo, NY, at home of TR's friend Ansley Wilcox	U.S. Federal District Judge John R. Hazel		—	inauguration of nation's youngest president
30th March 4, 1905	Theodore Roosevelt	Republican	46	Wash DC, East Portico	Chief Justice Melville W. Fuller	45°, sunny and windy	1	most colorful inaugural parade in history
31st March 4, 1909	William Howard Taft	Republican	51	Wash DC, U.S. Senate (d)	Chief Justice Melville W. Fuller	32°, snow	1	ceremony moved indoors due to blizzard; first time president and first lady rode together back to White House after ceremony
32nd March 4, 1913	Woodrow Wilson	Democratic	56	Wash, DC, East Portico	Chief Justice Edward D. White	55°, overcast	0	era of no inaugural balls begins

March 4, 1917	Woodrow Wilson	Democratic	60	Wash DC, Pres. Wilson's office at Capitol	Chief Justice Edward D. White		—	first private oath-taking on a Sunday
33rd March 5, 1917	Woodrow Wilson	Democratic	60	Wash DC, East Portico	Chief Justice Edward D. White	38°, partly cloudy and windy	0	first president to be sworn in two days in a row; first time women participated in inaugural parade
34th March 4, 1921	Warren G. Harding	Republican	55	Wash DC, East Portico	Chief Justice Edward D White	38°, sunny	0	first president to ride to inauguration in an automobile; first time loudspeakers used at inauguration ceremony
August 3, 1923	Calvin Coolidge	Republican	51	Plymouth Notch, VT, at home of CC's father	Col. John Coolidge, justice of the peace and notary public		—	oath administered by president's father
August 17, 1923	Calvin Coolidge	Republican	51	Wash DC, New Willard Hotel, CC's residence	Adolph A. Hoehling, justice of District of Columbia Supreme Ct.		—	took oath a second time to legitimize ceremony

INAUGURAL NUMBER AND DATE	PRESIDENT	PARTY	AGE	SITE OF INAUG.	SWORN IN BY	WEATHER	# OF INAUG. BALLS	NOTABLE ASPECTS
35th March 4, 1925	Calvin Coolidge	Republican	52	Wash DC, East Portico	Chief Justice William H. Taft	44°, sunny	0 (e)	first inauguration to be broadcast live on radio
36th March 4, 1929	Herbert Hoover	Republican	54	Wash DC, East Portico	Chief Justice William H. Taft	48°, rainy	0 (e)	first inauguration to be broadcast by sound newsreel
37th March 4, 1933	Franklin D. Roosevelt	Democratic	51	Wash DC, East Portico	Chief Justice Charles Evans Hughes	42°, mostly cloudy	1	"the only thing we have to fear is fear itself"
38th January 20, 1937	Franklin D. Roosevelt	Democratic	54	Wash DC, East Portico	Chief Justice Charles Evans Hughes	33°, cold and rainy	0	first Jan. 20 ceremony; first inauguration in which vice president was sworn in outside Capitol along with the president
39th January 20, 1941	Franklin D. Roosevelt	Democratic	58	Wash DC, East Portico	Chief Justice Charles Evans Hughes	29°, sunny and cold	0	first president to be elected to three terms in office

	Party	Age	Location	Chief Justice	Weather		Notes
40th January 20, 1945	Franklin D. Roosevelt	Democratic	62	Wash DC, White House South Portico	Chief Justice Harlan F. Stone	35°, snow before ceremony, then cloudy	0	because of World War, low-key inauguration held on White House balcony
April 12, 1945	Harry S. Truman	Democratic	60	Wash DC, White House Cabinet Room	Chief Justice Harlan F. Stone	64°, fair	—	first new president in more than twelve years
41st January 20, 1949	Harry S. Truman	Democratic	64	Wash DC, East Portico	Chief Justice Frederick M. Vinson	38°, sunny and windy	1	first televised inauguration
42nd January 20, 1953	Dwight D. Eisenhower	Republican	62	Wash DC, East Portico	Chief Justice Frederick M. Vinson	49°, cloudy	2	longest inaugural parade
January 20, 1957	Dwight D. Eisenhower	Republican	66	Wash DC, White House East Room	Chief Justice Earl Warren		—	private Sunday ceremony at White House
43rd January 21, 1957	Dwight D. Eisenhower	Republican	66	Wash DC, East Portico	Chief Justice Earl Warren	44°, mostly cloudy with snow flurries	4	inauguration of first president to be limited to two terms in office

INAUGURAL NUMBER AND DATE	PRESIDENT	PARTY	AGE	SITE OF INAUG.	SWORN IN BY	WEATHER	# OF INAUG. BALLS	NOTABLE ASPECTS
44th January 20, 1961	John F. Kennedy	Democratic	43	Wash DC, East Portico	Chief Justice Earl Warren	22°, snow before ceremony, then sunny and cold	5	"ask not what your country can do for you ..."; first time a poet participated in inauguration ceremony; first time both parents personally witnessed their son's inauguration
November 22, 1963	Lyndon B. Johnson	Democratic	55	Dallas, TX, aboard Air Force One	U.S. District Judge Sarah T. Hughes		—	only time president has been sworn in by a woman
45th January 20, 1965	Lyndon B. Johnson	Democratic	56	Wash DC, East Portico	Chief Justice Earl Warren	38°, cloudy with snow on ground	5	first lady held Bible during oath for first time

	President	Party	Age	Location	Oath administered by	Weather		Notes
46th January 20, 1969	Richard M. Nixon	Republican	56	Wash DC, East Portico	Chief Justice Earl Warren	35°, cloudy with rain and sleet later in day	6	first inaugural parade to be partially disrupted by protesters
47th January 20, 1973	Richard M. Nixon	Republican	60	Wash DC, East Portico	Chief Justice Warren E. Burger	42°, cloudy and windy	5	second inaugural parade to be partially disrupted by protesters
August 9, 1974	Gerald R. Ford	Republican	61	Wash DC, White House East Room	Chief Justice Warren E. Burger		—	first inauguration of someone never elected either president or vice president
48th January 20, 1977	Jimmy Carter	Democratic	52	Wash DC, East Portico	Chief Justice Warren E. Burger	28°, cold and sunny	7	only president to use a nickname when taking the formal oath; only president and first lady to walk entire length of inaugural parade route
49th January 20, 1981	Ronald Reagan	Republican	69	Wash DC, West Front	Chief Justice Warren E. Burger	55°, cloudy and mild	9	oldest president; first inauguration on Capitol's west side

INAUGURAL NUMBER AND DATE	PRESIDENT	PARTY	AGE	SITE OF INAUG.	SWORN IN BY	WEATHER	# OF INAUG. BALLS	NOTABLE ASPECTS
January 20, 1985	Ronald Reagan	Republican	73	Wash DC, at foot of White House grand staircase	Chief Justice Warren E. Burger		—	Sunday ceremony at White House
50th January 21, 1985	Ronald Reagan	Republican	73	Wash DC, Capitol Rotunda (d)	Chief Justice Warren E. Burger	7°, sunny but bitter cold (morning low:−4°)	9	ceremony moved indoors because of coldest weather ever for an inauguration; inaugural parade canceled
51st January 20, 1989	George Bush	Republican	64	Wash DC, West Front	Chief Justice William H. Rehnquist	51°, cloudy, mild and breezy	12	called inauguration "democracy's big day"
52nd January 20, 1993	William J. Clinton	Democratic	46	Wash DC, West Front	Chief Justice William H. Rehnquist	40°, sunny	11	first president to attend inaugural morning services at a predominantly African American church

53rd January 20, 1997	William J. Clinton	Democratic	50	Wash DC, West Front	Chief Justice William H. Rehnquist	34°, partly sunny and overcast	14	first inauguration broadcast live over the Internet; greatest number of inaugural balls
54th January 20, 2001	George W. Bush	Republican	54	Wash DC, West Front	Chief Justice William H. Rehnquist	36°, fog and rain, with sleet later in day	9 (f)	Father George became first for- mer president to personally witness the inauguration of his son; mother Barbara became first woman to personally witness the inauguration of both her hus- band and her son; first time a protest took place dur- ing the inaugural oath
55th January 20, 2005	George W. Bush	Republican	58	Wash DC, West Front	Chief Justice William H. Rehnquist	35°, mostly cloudy with some sun	10 (f)	first time a protest took place dur- ing the inaugural address

INAUGURAL NUMBER AND DATE	PRESIDENT	PARTY	AGE	SITE OF INAUG.	SWORN IN BY	WEATHER	# OF INAUG. BALLS	NOTABLE ASPECTS
56th January 20, 2009								

Note: Inauguration number in first column refers to the planned officially numbered ceremony, held every four years since 1789. Designations of "East Portico" and "West Front" refer to the east and west sides of the U.S. Capitol building. Weather information is from National Weather Service and refers to noontime temperature. Weather records are unofficial through 1869, and listed weather information pertains only to scheduled outdoor inaugurations.

(a) After oath on balcony of Federal Hall in 1789, Washington delivered his inaugural address before a joint session of Congress inside the Senate chamber.

(b) One week after the 1789 Inauguration, an inaugural ball was held at the New York Dancing Assemblies. Some historians have not recognized it as an inaugural ball because it was not planned as an official inauguration event.

(c) There was a small ball for members of Congress in 1793, but again, it was not an official inauguration event.

(d) Inauguration ceremony moved indoors because of poor weather in 1821, 1833, 1909 and 1985.

(e) There was a charity ball in 1925 and another in 1929.

(f) Figures for 2001 and 2005 include "Texas Black Tie and Boots Inaugural Ball," held the night before the inauguration ceremony.

References

About Women's History Web site.

Anderson, Judith Icke. *William Howard Taft: An Intimate History.* New York: W. W. Norton and Company, 1981.

Ambrose, Stephen E. *Nixon: The Triumph of a Politician 1962–1972.* New York: Simon and Schuster, 1989.

————. *Nixon: Ruin and Recovery 1973–1990.* New York: Simon and Schuster, 1991.

Barbee, David Rankin. "Inaugural Balls of the Past." 1933 *Inaugural Program.*

Bober, Natalie S. *Thomas Jefferson: Man on a Mountain.* New York: Atheneum, 1988.

Boykin, Edward. "Quizzing the Presidents." 1949 *Inaugural Program.*

Brendon, Piers. *Ike: His Life and Times.* New York: Harper and Row, 1986.

CBS *Evening News.* December 27, 2006.

Carroll, John Alexander, and Mary Wells Ashworth. *George Washington: First in Peace,* vol. 7. New York: Charles Scribner's Sons, 1957.

Carter, Jimmy. *Keeping Faith: Memoirs of a President.* New York: Bantam Books, 1982.

Clarke, Thurston. *Ask Not: The Inauguration of John F. Kennedy and the Speech That Changed America.* New York: Henry Holt and Company, 2004.

Coolidge, Calvin. *The Autobiography of Calvin Coolidge.* New York: Cosmopolitan Book Corporation, 1929.

Corbin, Michael. 2001. Hail to the Thief. *Baltimore City Paper.* January 24–30.

Davis, Burke. *Old Hickory: A Life of Andrew Jackson.* New York: Dial Press, 1977.

Durant, John, and Alice Durant. *Pictorial History of American Presidents.* New York: A. S. Barnes and Company, 1955.

Durbin, Louise. *Inaugural Cavalcade.* New York: Dodd, Mead and Company, 1971.

Eisenhower, Dwight D. *Mandate for Change.* Garden City, New York: Doubleday and Company, 1963.

Eisenhower, Julie Nixon. *Pat Nixon: The Untold Story.* New York: Simon and Schuster, 1986.

Epicenter Communications. *An American Reunion 1993: The 52nd Presidential Inauguration.* New York: Warner Books, 1993.

Essary, J. Fred. "The Passing of March Fourth." 1933 *Inaugural Program.*

Finney, Ruth. "Why a January 20th Inauguration?" 1937 *Inaugural Program.*

Fleming, Thomas. *The Man From Monticello: An Intimate Life of Thomas Jefferson.* New York: William Morrow and Company, 1969.

Freidel, Frank. *Franklin D. Roosevelt: Launching the New Deal.* Boston: Little, Brown and Company, 1973.

Goldstein, Matthew. "Myths of the Oath of Office." wash.org Web site, 2006.

Grollier. *The American Presidents.* Danbury, Connecticut: Grollier, Inc., 1992.

History News Network Web site, George Mason University.

Hurd, Charles. *A Treasury of Great American Speeches.* New York: Hawthorn Books, 1970.

Hurja, Emil Edward. *History of Presidential Inaugurations.* New York: New York Democratic Publishing Corporation, 1933.

Inaugural Committee. *A New Spirit, A New Commitment, A New America: The Inauguration of President Jimmy Carter.* New York: Bantam Books, 1977.

James, Marquis. *The Life of Andrew Jackson.* Indianapolis: Bobbs-Merrill, 1938.

Johnson, Lady Bird. *A White House Diary.* Austin, Texas: Holt Rinehart and Winston, 1970.

Kittler, Glenn D. *Hail to the Chief!* Philadelphia: Chilton Company, 1965.

Library of Congress Web site (www.loc.gov)

Lindley, Ernest K. "The Presidency, Then and Now." 1949 *Inaugural Program.*

Lindop, Edmond. *Presidents by Accident.* New York: Franklin Watts, 1991.

Lingo, Jane Tunstall. "Inaugural Balls of Former Days." 1949 *Inaugural Ball Program.*

Lomask, Milton. *"I Do Solemnly Swear ..."*: *The Story of the Presidential Inauguration*. New York: Ariel Books, 1966.

McCoy, Donald R. *Calvin Coolidge: The Quiet President*. New York: Macmillan Company, 1967.

McCullough, David. *John Adams*. New York: Simon and Schuster, 2001.

Morgan, George. *The Life of James Monroe*. New York: AMS Press, 1921.

Oates, Stephen B. *With Malice Toward None*. New York: Harper and Row, 1977.

Pauley, Matthew A. *I Do Solemnly Swear: The President's Constitutional Oath: Its Meaning and Importance in the History of Oaths*. Lanham, Maryland: United Press of America, Inc., 1999.

Parmet, Herbert S. *George Bush: The Life of a Lone Star Yankee*. New York: Lisa Drew/Scribner, 1997.

Perret, Geoffrey. *Ulysses S. Grant: Soldier and President*. New York: Random House, 1997.

Phillips, Cabel. *The Truman Presidency: The History of a Triumphant Succession*. New York: Macmillan Company, 1966.

Phillips, Louis. *Ask Me Anything About the Presidents*. New York: Avon Books, 1992.

Polk, James K. March 5, 1849, diary entry. "I Do Solemnly Swear," Library of CongressWeb site.

Public Broadcasting System Web site: "The Inaugural Classroom."

Quarles, Benjamin. *Lincoln and the Negro*. New York: Oxford University Press, 1962.

Reagan, Nancy. *My Turn*. New York: Random House, 1989.

Remini, Robert V. *Andrew Jackson and the Course of American Freedom 1822–1832.* New York: Harper and Row, 1981.

————. *Andrew Jackson and the Course of American Democracy 1833–1845.* New York: Harper and Row, 1984.

Roney, Joan. Interview. dc.indymedia.org. Web site, 2001.

Rubel, David. *Mr. President.* Alexandria, Virginia: Time-Life Books, 1998.

Rupp, Robert. C-SPAN interview at West Virginia Wesleyan College, 1999.

Sandburg, Carl. *The War Years.* New York: Harcourt Brace & Company, 1939.

Smith, Gene. *High Crimes and Misdemeanors: The Impeachment and Trial of Andrew Johnson.* New York: Morrow, 1977.

Sobel, Robert. *Coolidge: An American Enigma.* Washington: Regnery Publishing, Inc., 1998.

Tibbits, Alison Davis. *James K. Polk.* Springfield, New Jersey: Enslow Publishers, 1999.

TIME. An Old Man's Memory. March 25, 1929.

TIME. The Thirty-Second. April 23, 1945.

Truman, Harry S. *Mr. Citizen.* New York: Bernard Geis Associates, 1953.

United States Capitol Historical Society. *We, The People: The Story of the United States Capitol.* Washington: National Geographic Society, 1978.

United States Congress. *The Capitol: A Pictorial History of the Capitol and of the Congress.* U.S. Government Printing Office, 1979.

United States Constitution: Twelfth Amendment, 1804; Twentieth Amendment, 1933, Twenty-second Amendment, 1951.

Walker, Ernest George. "Inaugural Parades of Other Days." 1933 *Inaugural Program.*

Walworth, Arthur. *Woodrow Wilson.* Boston: Houghton Mifflin Company, 1965.

Wikander, Lawrence E. "The Second Oath." *The Real Calvin Coolidge.* Plymouth Notch, Vermont: Calvin Coolidge Memorial Foundation, 1998.

Acknowledgments

The author wishes to thank the following people who graciously contributed to this project. These individuals' assistance included taking time for interviews, answering questions about the past, and helping with photography and graphics.

Bill Allen, Architect of the Capitol

Bill Allen, U.S. Senate Photo Studio Manager (yes, another Bill Allen!)

Claudia Anderson, Lyndon B. Johnson Presidential Library

Cindy Bendat

Jason Bendat

Robert Bohannon, Jimmy Carter Presidential Library

Sharon Culley, National Archives and Records Administration

Debbie Carter, George Bush Presidential Library

Jodie Evans

Jules Garfunkel, St. John's Masonic Lodge, New York City

Tony Guzzi, The Hermitage

Hon. Alan M. Hantman, Architect of the Capitol

Bill Jenney, Vermont Historical Society

Donald R. Kennon, United States Historical Society

Greg Miller

Kimberly Norco, Massachusetts Historical Society

SFC Richard Ruddle, The Old Fife and Drum Corps, United States Army

Elizabeth Safly, Harry S. Truman Presidential Library

Matt Schaefer, Herbert Hoover Presidential Library

Lynn Smith, Herbert Hoover Presidential Library

Kathy Struss, Dwight D. Eisenhower Presidential Library

Pauline Testerman, Harry S. Truman Presidential Library

Piers A. Vaughan, St. John's Masonic Lodge, New York City

About the Author

Jim Bendat graduated from Northwestern University and Loyola Law School and has been a lawyer with the Los Angeles County Public Defender's office since 1978. His works have appeared in the *New Republic, Los Angeles Times, Chicago Tribune, San Francisco Chronicle,* and *Baltimore Sun,* and he covered the 1990 NCAA Final Four and three NBA Finals for Reuters. Since his first publication on presidential inauguration history in 2000, he has been featured as an inaugural historian by all of the major networks in the United States, as well as in Canada and the United Kingdom. He worked as a correspondent at the last two inaugurations, for MSNBC in 2001 and British network ITV in 2005.

Index